THE SPOOKSTER

.Plus
A Short Story

A CRIME THRILLER NOVEL

By:

Orvillo Ricks

TABLE OF CONTENTS

COPYRIGHT@2021................... 3

PROLOGUE 4

THE TEENAGER 41

THE YOUNG ADULT 92

THE ADULT 111

THE WAXSTER 120

I LIKE IT HERE 164

THE TRADE 169

PAUL AND DAWN 221

COPYRIGHT@2021

All **Rights** Reserved

Copyright Registration Number:
TXu 2-278-829

Copyright date:
Septembter 27, 2021

Self-Edited & Self Published

Via Amazon Kdp
77archtony@gmail.com

PROLOGUE

Many people in this country really don't know the significance of the C.I.A. Not only do they protect our interests abroad, they also do so at home, clandestinely, when needed too, especially with criminals that are above and beyond normal channels financially, As well as mentally...

A serial killer called "The Waxter," was on the loose and terrorizing the nation with his murderous crime spree to the degree that outside influences are needed to quell the violence. Without looking up from his desk the President said, "Assign Special Agent Dash to the "Waxter" case, he'll round' em up," said the President.
"Yes, sir" replied Director Foss of the C.I.A. and got on the phone.

(Circa 2009)

THE YOUNGSTER

Willis Dash was 11 years old, but he looked like he was 7. He was very small for his age. His father was an air force pilot currently stationed at Plattsburgh air force base in Plattsburgh, New York, where Willis was going. Willis loved airplanes and had twenty hours of flying time logged unofficially. This was a secret only he and his father shared. His father, Captain Dwayne Dash, had rented flying time with a twin-engine turboprop last summer and took his beloved son Willis up with him and taught him the dynamics of the aircraft and the art of flying a plane. Willis was a smart boy, very smart. Smarter than most boys his age, his aptitude for learning was above average. Even though he was eleven, he was scheduled to take the G.E.D. in the fall. But for now, he could only think about returning to New York to his father, so he could resume his flying lessons. He also planned to join the air force and be a pilot like his dad when he was of age.

The Boeing triple seven out of Miami international took off flawlessly, heading for New York. As soon as the seat belt sign went inert, Willis got up and ran to the middle of the plane to have a look at the wing, hoping to see some flap movement of the ailerons, he was too late though, the plane had already achieved its cruising altitude of thirty-five thousand feet, and the ailerons were still and leveled off. Not one to be put off by such a minor setback, Willis continued inspecting the plane. He went to the galley to see the stewardesses. They were nice to him when boarding and also very pretty, and he felt that his best chance to get a tour of the cockpit lay with them, and he desperately wanted to get into, and look over that cockpit, and talk about airmanship with the captain and co-pilots.

After talking and exuding his boyish charms on the stewardesses, they agreed to take him to the cockpit for a tour, but it would have to be after the inflight meal and drinks, which they set out to do. As soon as they went to it, his curiosity got the best of him. He opened the pantry cabinet door and peered in. It was roomy. Instantly it became his secret hideaway. He squeezed his little frame inside, and no sooner than he'd done so three men came in the galley area. He pulled the door almost shut, and they started talking.

"In exactly ten minutes, the gas will deploy. Make sure you have your masks on-here," said the speaker, and opened the galley cabinet right above where Willis hid, pulled out three brown paper bags, gave one to each man, kept one for himself. The leader started speaking again:
"You stay right here; you go amid ship and, as planned, I'll go to the cockpit. Synchronize watches again." They looked at their watches, Willis looked at the men through the crack in the slightly ajar door. He was no expert on nationality, but these men looked European, eastern bloc Slavs, he thought. "Okay," repeated the leader, "When you hear the beep; you have 30 seconds to mask up; good luck."

Two of the men left to assume their positions, with the third standing there waiting. Willis looked around the cramped compartment frantically, for something he could cover his face with. He only saw a small metal bar about 8" long. He grabbed the bar out of pure fear, and he was literally scared to even move; he was frozen in fear, praying the man didn't open the pantry door and look in and find him. Then the dreaded beeping sounded. The bells at church never sounded that loud, thought Willis. Then he heard the unmistakable sound of the uncrumpling of the brown bag being opened. Willis opened the door and peeped out. The man was pulling out a black oxygen mask, his back was to Willis. Willis reached out and snatched the mask out of the man's hands, darted backward, pulled the pantry door shut, and slid the 8" bar he found between the lock and the door jammed, locking himself in securely. The man kicked the door wildly in a vain attempt to get it open, but it wasn't working. Willis put the mask on. The man tried to use a galley knife to pry the door back far enough to get his fingers between the frame, but the knife broke. The sharpened edge fell inside to Willis. The man started kicking the door wildly again in a vain attempt to get it open. The door bent inwards enough so he could use his hands to try to pull it open, and when he did, Willis started stabbing him in his hands with the broken galley knife tip. He released his grip and fell backward on the floor, holding his hands and moaning as he succumbed to the fumes. A few minutes went by, and silence enveloped the galley. The only sound Willis could hear was the muted hum of the engines. The man lay on his stomach with his hands underneath him dead. Willis stepped out and looked for a few more minutes at the dead man, then heard one of the other men yell something.

He got on the floor, looked down the aisle, and saw the other man going from seat to seat, apparently checking to see if anyone was still alive. The man also had his mask off. He called out "Restov," again to his accomplice and got no answer and started moving faster; Willis took off the mask, put it back on the dead man, re-entered the pantry cabinet, and re-locked himself back inside. After a few minutes, the other man came, and Willis heard him, "Restov? shit, his mask must be defective, shit, shit, shit!" he said. It's a good thing the man was on his stomach Willis thought, otherwise, the other man might have seen his hands and knew something was up. Willis heard the man leaving and came out again. He couldn't stay here; he had to do something. He had to find a better hiding place; he had to.

E.T.A.: New York, 90 Minutes

Willis silently slid out of his hiding place with his bar and looked down the aisle from ground level. He could see clear to the cockpit. One of the men stood facing forward and gesturing with his hands, evidently conversing with the other man sitting in the pilot's seat. He looked around the galley to find a better weapon and could only find more knives. He took one and stuffed it in between his belt and pants loop. Out of the clear blue sky, he was hungry, found some granola bars, and started munching. Then the thought came to him; he had to get someone's cell phone and call his father at his base to let him know what was happening. He Looked down the aisle, ready to dash down it to check some of the bodies for a cell phone; there had to be one on somebody. He peeked down the aisle again from ground level and saw the man with his back to him and a phone to his ear; turning around, he stepped back and waited. He heard the man talking and his voice getting closer! He went to a bathroom and stepped inside, but he grabbed the mini fire extinguisher off the wall before he did. The man's voice became louder; he was right outside the bathroom door - Willis was deathly scared. He quietly put the fire extinguisher on the floor and pulled out the knife. If the man opened the door, he would stab him in the heart, just as his father had shown him. He stood stock still, scared to death, as the man walked up, talking on his phone.

"Yes, Pasha, we are 75 minutes out, go according to plan, have the police uniforms waiting as planned," then silence, "Pasha, you are a police officer, they will believe you, just make sure of the diversion and be amongst the first to enter the plane okay, see you then." Then Willis heard the adjoining bathroom door open. Willis picked up the fire extinguisher, opened his door quietly, and stood on the lip of the toilet seat with the fire extinguisher held high above his head. The toilet next door flushed, and the man stepped out and walked by Willis' toilet. Willis didn't hesitate. He jumped forward and swung the fire extinguisher with all his might. It hit the man behind his right ear solidly with a loud thump. The man's knees buckled immediately, and he fell forward, haphazardly, on drunken legs, down to one knee, dazed but not out, bleeding. Willis immediately hit him again, and he fell flat on his face. Willis hit him again for good measure, and he was out cold. Willis then grabbed the knife and did what his father taught him to incapacitate a threat. He pushed the knife just above the waist through the man's spine, paralyzing him. He cut his tweed shirt into long strips and tied his hands to his feet with a midshipman's knot with a double half hitch. Something he learned from the boy scouts. He then gagged him with the rest of the shirt and pulled his body out of view of the aisle. He took the man's phone out of his pocket and was about to call when he realized he had to incapacitate the other man before he realized his partner was missing. He knew he had to take the other guy out while he had his back to the aisle looking forward in the cockpit. He knew he couldn't face the man straight up, so he didn't waste time making any call because if the man came while he was doing it, he would kill him for what he'd already done. He put the phone in his pocket, grabbed the fire extinguisher, and ran up the aisle at full speed.

The cockpit door was wide open. The man sat in the pilot's seat monitoring the instruments when Willis came up from behind, swung the fire extinguisher with all his might, and hit him on the right side of his head, right on the temple. The man slumped over, unconscious immediately. Willis went to work quickly. He pulled him to the cockpit floor, snipped his spinal cord, and tied him up just the same as the other one. He looked at the instrument panel, and the lighted auto pilot sign was on. He breathed a sigh of relief. Then he stood stock still for a moment to get his thoughts together. And when he did, he picked up the headsets, put them on, and began speaking.
"Mayday, Mayday, mayday; this is flight 1504. Does anyone read me?"
"This is Atlanta International 1504; what's the problem, over?"

"Copy, I read you, loud and clear," replied Willis.

"We have you on radar 1504; what's your problem, over?"

"I don't know how to land this thing; that's the problem, over?" replied Willis.

"1504, who are you, why are you in the cockpit, and what's the problem over?"

"My name is Willis Dash, sir; I'm 11 years old. Hijackers took over the plane and I've incapacitated them. The plane is on autopilot - I don't know how to land it." The controllers at Atlanta International tower were stunned. Silence enveloped the entire tower as everyone heard the entire exchange. The shift supervisor picked up the mike calmly and said:

"1504, can you get one of the adults in the cockpit?"

"No sir," replied Willis.

"1504, I thought you said the hijackers were incapacitated?"

"Yes, sir, they are tied, bound, and gagged."

"Then why can't you get an adult in the cockpit, 1504?"

"Because they are all dead, sir." Replied Willis with deep sorrow in his voice. The tower couldn't believe what they were hearing; they stood in shocked stunned silence, but what they did believe was his low and painful crying.

"They're all dead, 1504?" asked control.
"Yes, sir, all 310 passengers, sir," replied Willis.
"How did you survive 1504?" asked the controller.
"By hiding, sir," answered Willis.
"What's your name, and can you please call me Willis" asked Willis.
"Yes, I can call you Willis. My name is Carlton Parks, head controller here, and we're going to get you home safe and in one-piece, okay Willis?" he replied.
"I have twenty hours of flying time, sir." replied Willis.
"Really? That's great, Willis, and will help us get you down," he said.
"My father is an air force pilot stationed at Plattsburgh, sir. Can you patch me through to him, please?" asked Willis.
"He's an air force pilot?" he asked gleefully.
"Yes, sir, I know that if you notify Plattsburgh of a hijacked plane, they'll scramble two jets to intercept, and he will be one of them; I'm sure this is his tour; if he doesn't come one of the others will, I know them all sir," replied Willis.
"That's right, Willis, I must do that and, in the meantime, while I go to it, I want you to talk to Jimmy, who's sitting right here next to me listening, okay? He's going to give you in-flight systems check; read the instruments

to him that he asks, and don't panic, we'll get you down safely, Willis," said Parks.
"Okay, sir, will do, over and out," replied Willis.

Carlton Parks leaned back as Jimmy took over talking to Willis and said to himself, "Jesus H. Fucking Christ. Three hundred ten dead, and an 11-year-old boy at the helm." He picked up the phone and notified the air force, Homeland Security, the F.B.I., and the N.Y.P.D. of the impending situation that was about to unfold. He also thought to himself that's one hell of a kid up there.

* * * * * * * * *

E.T.A.: New York, 55 Minutes

LaGuardia Airport in Elmhurst, Queens, New York, was bustling with activity. Emergency service crews were everywhere, getting ready for the imminent arrival of flight 1504. The fire department and Police were also there in full force. No one knew exactly what was going on with the flight; they were just getting ready for an emergency landing.

Two air force jets were already airborne when the alarm was raised of the hijacked plane. Captain Dwayne Dash was in the officers' mess when he was paged and summoned to the squad commander's office.

"Sir, you wanted to see me?" he said, saluting smartly.

"A dire situation has arisen in which you will play an integral part, so skip the formalities," he said.

"Yes, sir," replied Captain Dash.

"Flight 1504 out of Miami had been hijacked. The hijackers have been, I was told, incapacitated by an 11-year-old boy named Willis Dash, who is asking for his father-you." Captain Dwayne Dash attempted to cut in but was cut off by his commander, who continued. "According to your son, he has incapacitated the hijackers and is in control of the plane. He says all the passengers are dead. When asked how that happened, he said he would only be debriefed by his father and that his father would help him land the plane. Your orders are as follows: You and tiger two are to intercept, escort, and make sure your boy lands that plane in one piece. Coordinates will be given to you in flight so git, and God speed, and good luck." In less than five minutes, Tigers one and two were airborne, headed south to intercept and escort the plane.

* * * * * * * * *

The first jet fighters that were rerouted to intercept and escort pulled alongside the triple seven gracefully. Flight 1504 was now being handled by LaGuardia International, who advised Willis of the frequency band for the fighters, and he switched over while they listened in.
"1504, this Raven one and two on your port and starboard side over," said one of the Airforce jets that pulled up alongside of the Boeing.
"Copy that raven one and two; you guys look sleek over there. I can't wait to fly one of the things myself; who exactly am I speaking to?"
"Captain T.J. Brooks and McNamara, over,"
"T.J., it's me, T.J., Willis, Captain Dash's son, over," said Willis eagerly.
"What the hell is going on, Willis? Are you okay? Talk to me, over?" replied T.J.
"I'm fine, T.J. you got to help me land this thing. Can you get my dad for me, T.J.?" asked Willis.
"He's on his way, Willis; you just stay calm; we will get you down safely, okay, over?" said T.J.
"Roger that T.J. I can't tell you what's going on because I rightly don't know, and I don't know who's listening in, so I'm assuming the

worst and keeping a lid on it like dad always says," said Willis.

"Okay, Willis, roger that, let's do in-flight systems check till your dad gets here, okay?" replied T.J.

"Cool," said Willis.

* * * * * * * * *

"Somehow or another, an 11-year-old boy is flying the plane, comrade." Said one man to another over a phone.

"So, to your saying we need to abort Pasha?" asked the other man.

"Yes, immediately."

"I don't have to tell you that you must get his phone, do I?" said the man.

"No, comrade, I will retrieve it; I will be amongst the first to board the plane if it lands safely."

"See that you do or else...." said the other man angrily, hanging up the phone.

* * * * * * * * *

Homeland Security Director Katheryn Moore had to be the sharpest tool in the shed because of the assumptions she was making to herself. She was in a hangar along with an array of law enforcement people who were waiting for flight 1504's arrival.

Everyone there was sitting in front of laptops, viewing security footage of everyone boarding the plane in Miami. She had one thing on her laptop that everyone else didn't. Top secret clearance for Facial recognition software of military personnel, the world over, courtesy of the C.I.A. As she watched the footage, three of the men boarding stood out to her because they appeared to board separately, and their bearing appeared formal in a military type of way. She tagged them individually, found no match for their American names with their faces anywhere, and entered them in the military facial recognition software program...

Pasha Yebnenko was worried and in a quandary. How the hell does an 11-year-old boy have control of the plane. What the hell happened up there? All was going according to plan when he last spoke to Demtri. Now all hell's breaking loose. He had to beg his superior to be a part of the boarding team, and now as they were checking their equipment in preparation, he was sweating profusely with fear. His family's lives were at stake back home in Crimea, and his brothers, who were fighting in Chechnya, depended on him, and now this. Failure on the part of Demtri might not bode well for him. He had to get that phone. Why didn't Demetri just take one from one of the passengers once they had control of the plane? What went wrong up there, he wondered.

Special Agent Connor Rawlings of the F.B.I. shared a dim view of everyone and anyone who didn't work for the bureau. He especially did not like working with the N.Y.P.D. because of their shoot first and let the local D.A. work it out later policy; they made all law enforcement entities look bad, and the people they were there to help and protect didn't trust them and feared them instead of feeling safe and secure in their presence. The N.Y.P.D. thought they were God's gift to truth, justice, law enforcement, and the American way.

But right now, he couldn't let his prejudices interfere with the matter at hand. His bosses were highly upset with the current situation and wanted answers last week. He would also be amongst the first to board the plane. As he was prepping his equipment, he couldn't help but wonder about the Homeland Security agent, Katheryn Moore. She was a real looker. The word was that she was very smart, so smart they called her special agent E.S.P. She had to be intelligent to hold the position she held. What caught Rawlings, though, was her beauty; she was uncommonly pretty, and he noticed that even though the situation was grave, all the men here seemed taken in by her in one way or another, but she seemed completely oblivious to that fact. He wanted to marry her! this was crazy, he thought to himself; I need to focus on the matter at hand. So, he turned away in disgust with himself; that's why he didn't notice officer Pasha Yebnemkos' obvious nervousness, the furtive way he moved, or the phone call he made.

* * * * * * * * *

"Dad is that you?" asked Willis.
"Yes, son, are you okay?" asked his father as his jet pulled alongside of the big Boeing triple 7.
"Yes, especially now that you are here," replied Willis.
"That's right, son, you're good, and we'll get you home in one piece in no time," stated his father.
"Mommy will be worried dad when the story hits the news wire," said Willis.
"Yes, but we're going to be okay, got it?" said his father strongly.
"Yes, dad," replied Willis imitating his father's strong voice as best he could.
"Good. What we're going to do is continue your flying lessons son," said his father.

"Okay, dad," replied Willis.
"Then you're going to land this thing," said his father confidently.
"Yes dd," replied Willis.
"First, I want you to program a new course into the autopilot controller," said his father.
"Where are we going, dad?" asked Willis.
"Out to sea son," answered his father.
"Why?" he asked.
"So, you can fly the plane at low-level altitude without hitting any buildings," replied his father.
"Okay, dad, what's the course," he said.
"Type in 2-2-5, son, and feel the plane, son. Get a feel for the plane. Put your hands on the yoke and your feet on the rudder pedals, but don't obstruct them," said his father.
"Got it, new course plotted," replied Willis.

The big, oversized triple-seven started changing course and veering east-northeast gracefully. Willis felt the plane's power and loved every second of it, caught in the euphoria of flying in the cockpit of the big triple seven.

* * * * * * * * *

Katherine Moore's laptop pinged three consecutive times and showed each of the men she had tagged for identification. Two were Chechen rebels, and the third was a Crimean special forces operator. She knew these men were the ones who attempted to take the plane but was at a loss as to why. She transferred the information to an S.D. card and gave it to the others. Connor Rawlings wondered how she had access to such sensitive information, and he didn't when she forwarded the information to him. Pasha Yebnemko looked over the shoulder of his commanding officer at the pictures on his laptop, visibly shuddered, and became a shade paler. Katheryn Moore saw his reaction and immediately pulled up his dossier from her files.

* * * * * * * * *

With great trepidation, Dwayne Dash gave his son the green light to disengage the autopilot and take control of the plane, having him read one gauge after another to him, so he knew how the plane was responding in free flight. Everything seemed fine. Now came the hard part, turning the plane back towards land. He could have easily instructed Willis to have the autopilot do it, but he wanted him to get the feel of the plane and of controlling it. When landing, he needed these attributes in the event of cross winds and downdrafts to help compensate for the craft's levelness.

"Okay, Willis, time to turn her on your own a couple of times... Do exactly as I showed you in the turboprop plane- make sure you turn the yoke the opposite way of the rudder pedal you will use, watch your turn indicator, and go no more than thirty degrees. On my mark, now, son." Willis did exactly as he was told, and the craft responded to his touch admirably. The advancement in aviation technologies made it easy to fly a plane once you get a feel for it; the hard part was sticking the landing. Willis completed the turn with glee and straightened the craft back up with ease. Willis was a natural, his father thought, as he watched the plane and its handling. They repeated the exercise several times and dumped excess fuel in the process.

Willis heard a dragging sound, looked over his shoulder, and saw the man he knocked out by the bathroom dragging himself forward, bloody head and all. Somehow or another, he had gotten free of his bonds. He must not have tied them tight enough, he thought. "Dad, got to go, man on the loose." As he was taking off the headset, he heard his dad yell something but ignored him. The pilot was awake but looked groggy, like he didn't know where he was. Willis picked up the fire extinguisher, checked the pilot's binds to ensure he wouldn't get loose, and stepped out of the cockpit towards the oncoming man.

"So, you couldn't stay put, huh?" Willis said as he walked up and stopped in front of the man looking down at him.

"You and your whole family will die for this unless you let me go now- I Promise you that," he said.

"You and your cronies killed everyone on board, and you think for a minute that I'm going to set you free so you could kill me too?" said Willis.

"Think about saving your family then; once your name is known, they're all dead," he said.

"Since you are making useless threats, let me make a real one for you. I have your phone, stupid, and the N.S.A. will track every last one of you through it." With all his might, Willis then swung down with lightning speed and smashed the man's outstretched hand with the fire extinguisher, the man screamed horrendously in pain and pulled his hand to his body, holding it with his other hand. Willis grabbed his other hand, pinned it down with his feet, and smashed those fingers. The man screamed so loud his father could probably hear it from outside across the sky. "You want to threaten my family?"

said Willis and yanked his head back by his hair and swung a short chopping blow that knocked out his two top teeth, then did it again knocking out his bottom four. Then he broke his nose, and the man went unconscious. He retied him thoroughly this time and went back to the cockpit. He looked down at the other man, who seemed incoherent.

"Those screams bought you out of it, huh?" said Willis.

"Tell me what you want, and I'll see to it that your family gets it- that's my word as a man," he said with a thick slavish accent. "But you must release me; we can say I was hurt when I helped you subdue the others."

"Sounds good. Can you get me a Mig-29 Foxbat?" Willis said as he retook the pilot's seat, put the headset halfway on again, and started calling his dad.

"Dad, come in, dad."

"Are you okay, son?"

"Yes sir, all clear over here."

"Okay, son, you had me worried."

"Combatant incapacitated, sir."

"Okay, we'll be making our run to New York Now."

"Okay, dad. If I don't make it, daddy, I love you, and tell mommy I love her too."

"Don't worry, son; you'll make it and be able to tell her yourself."

Willis then got up quickly and swung the fire extinguisher, knocked out the pilot's front teeth, and then battered his elbows to smithereens. He passed out again, and Willis hit him on the nose, breaking it.

Somehow or another, the media got word of the impending crash landing and were out in force as the triple seven came into land. As the back Wheels hit the tarmac on the left side first and the plane jolted to the right, and those wheels touched down: making the plane bounce up, Willis pushed the thrusters forward and down, flapped the ailerons, and the plane went up and airborne again.
"Dad, the horizon indicator is off on the left side," said Willis.
"That was scary, son, but you managed it well; I'm proud of you and I know you'll land it well on the next go around, compensate for it, Willis," said his father.

Meanwhile, on the ground, it was palpable fear as everyone watched the plane bounce and take back off amid countless "oh my Gods" being said. Pasha Yebnemko thought, hopefully, that the plane would crash and burn and destroy the phone and watched intently as the plane circled twice more and then came in again. This time though, Willis watched the horizon- indicator and said to himself, 'use the force Willis' and tipped the left-wing one degree above the horizon indicator on the left side and both wheels touched down at the same time, and his father said, "nose down, now Willis," and he did it. "Yes, Willis," said his father gleefully in his headset, and Willis smiled broadly.

"Dad, I'm not being debriefed by no one until you get here, I have something to tell you first."

"Okay, son, I'll be there in 90 minutes' tops, and I'll have my commander radio in that you are not to be questioned."

"Roger that," said Willis.

"Over and out," said his father, and Willis watched as the escort fighters headed north towards Plattsburgh to their base. Then the terminal chimed in for Willis to follow the emergency service vehicle across the tarmac, and he did.

Everyone in the tower was ecstatic at what they had just witnessed. And had their own thoughts about it. An eleven-year-old boy had just made a perfect three-point landing. Wow! Katheryn Moore was wondering at the intellect of the boy on the plane, what he did was no mean feat, first he somehow subdued three hijackers, and now he's landed the biggest commercial plane we have to date.

Connor Rawlings was thinking this must be some kind of super kid, a prodigy of some sort and made a mental note took look up the boy's father's files... Pasha Yebnemko was sweating bullets. The media was going to have a frenzy when they found out the pilot was an eleven-year-old boy! But what they wouldn't digest so soundly when they found out was the body count.

* * * * * * * * *

Flight 1504 taxied down the runway with numerous emergency service vehicles in pursuit. As it entered the hangar and came to a halt, the hangar door was shut, the rolling staircase was put in place, and the swat team went up with precision for a tactical entry. Willis opened the door, and they stormed in and went down the aisle with arms raised, ready to shoot, but there was no one to shoot. One cop, in particular, did no such thing, though; he went straight to the men tied up and started frisking them. Then he asked Willis, "Where's the other one?" Willis pointed towards the back, and he started frisking the dead man's body; at this point Willis was whisked away.

Katheryn Moore took one look at Willis, and even though she prided herself on the fact that she never let her feelings play a significant role in her work, she couldn't do so now; her motherly instincts took over. This youngster was a very handsome kid, and without saying a word, Willis won her heart with his smile.

"Hello, young man, my name is Special Agent Katheryn Moore from Homeland Security. How are you feeling? Do you need medical assistance?" she asked.

"Yes, I need C.P.R., would you please give it to me?" responded Willis. His comment got a big smile from her and laughter all around the room. This lady, and that's what she was, was very pretty, no doubt about it, Willis thought to himself. He'd have to be careful not to let her sway information from him. At this point, he did not know who to trust. Willis still had the knife in his belt loop and the fire extinguisher in his right hand as he looked around the room filled with Laughter. A man stepped forward with his hand extended for a handshake and said, "My name is Connor Rawlings, F.B.I., glad to meet you, Willis, you're a brave man." Willis looked at his outstretched hand, then looked him in the face and didn't say a word. The N.Y. P. D. liaison Sgt. Calvin Cook stepped forward and said, "Hi, my name is Sgt. Calvin Cook, N.Y.P.D., and I understand you've just gone through a very stressful ordeal, and I want you to know we are all here for you and to help you. You can trust us; why don't you let me have that knife?" and reached his hand forward. Willis raised the fire extinguisher to hit him, and he backed up and said, "Willis, we're on your side. You can trust us."

"No, I can't; I don't trust you as far as I can throw you, which isn't very far. You guys shoot and kill innocent unarmed civilians, and don't do a day in jail for the nefarious act. Those are not the acts of trustworthy people, so if it's all the same to you, I'll keep my knife and I'll trust you to know that I know how to use it, now back up away from me and don't come near me."

Everyone went silent and looked at the little boy and knew that he had just gone through a harrowing ordeal and so thought him traumatized by it. Connor Rawlings immediately knew this was no ordinary kid. He just subdued three hijackers, landed a Boeing Triple 777, the biggest passenger aircraft in the world, and was smart enough to know not to trust the N.Y.P.D. He's my kind of kid he thought. Katheryn Moore's phone beeped, and she answered and listened, then turned around and said, "I've just received a direct order from the Joint Chiefs of Staff. Per National Security, no one, and I mean no one, is to question Willis about anything until his father gets here, E.T.A. 70 minutes, is that clear?" With that, everyone turned to process the plane even though they were craving details of how Willis took control of it.

    Willis sat at the makeshift desk of Katheryn Moore, looking at her. She stopped what she was doing, looked at him, and asked, "Are you okay?" very concerned. Willis sensed her sincerity and replied in kind, "Yes, Ma'am."
"Want to talk?" she asked.
"Yes, but let's wait for dad. I'm not going to say what happened twice," he replied.
"You're smart," she said.
"You're pretty," he replied.
"Thank you, Willis, for your very handsome yourself," she said sincerely looking at him.
"I can tell by the symmetry of your face, the look in your eyes, that you are smarter than all of them," he said.
"So are you," she said.
"We haven't even talked, in detail, about anything, but I sense you understand the depth of my intellect. The only other people who truly understand are my parents."
"I even looked you up," she said.
"You look everyone up, typical woman," said Willis, and she laughed.

"I'll share with you if you share with me," said Willis. She stopped and looked at him.

"I'll give you any information you want, but I will ask no question of you as I've been directed not to," she said.

"You are very intelligent; you know exactly what I'm getting at," he said.

"What do you want to know?" she asked.

"The names of the swat team members that boarded the plane," she raised an eyebrow, turned to her laptop, and started typing. After a few clicks, she turned the Laptop towards Willis. He looked at the names intently. "This one, can I get a printout?" he asked. She looked at the name and said, "That's very interesting, and yes, you can get a printout," tapped a couple of times, and the printer hummed to life. "Why is that name interesting, as you put it?" asked Willis, and she explained how he seemed worried and became preoccupied when he saw the photos of the men, she had tagged that boarded the plane. She handed him the dossier of Pasha Yebnemko as soon as it came off the printer. As Willis read it, he remembered the man he had subdued was talking to someone named Pasha.

Pasha Yebnemko came strolling across the hangar with purpose towards where Willis sat. Willis looked up, saw him, put the paperwork face down, and said, "Ms. Moore, may I see your gun?" She looked up, surprised by the request, but then saw Yebnemko headed their way.

"Willis, you know I can't do that," she said.

"Then pull it out, so he knows you got one too," said Willis.

"I'll need the fire extinguisher and the knife; they are evidence in this investigation,"

said Yebnemko, firmly looking at Willis when he walked up. He never once looked at Agent Moore.

"You'll get it the same way those guys on the plane got it," said Willis. Yebnemko was seething mad. His right hand was held negligently by his gun. This man was like a cobra ready to strike.

"I'm not asking you," he said.

"Good, just remember I told you exactly how you're going to get it," said Willis not blinking an eye.

"Officer, he's just been through a traumatic ordeal and not to be questioned or pressured in any way, a direct order from the pentagon, so, officer, you can go about processing the plane. You will receive the knife and fire extinguisher in due time; goodbye," she said with authority, he looked at her then back at Willis then stalked off angrily.

"Ms. Moore?" said Willis as he walked off.

"Yes, Willis?" she asked.

"You need to pull some strings right now," said Willis.

"What do you want me to do?" she said.

"Have the N.S.A. recordings of his phone conversations reviewed for his involvement in the hijacking scheme and get a search warrant for his place. You need to do that right now, or else he might get away." She got on the phone. Willis called Connor Rawlings. "Mr. Rawlings, you must put a tail on N.Y.P.D. officer Pash Yebnemko. He is and has played an integral part in the hijacking of flight 1504 and the subsequent deaths that occurred. You must assign agents to watch his house, relatives, and friends, as he is a Ukraine nationalist, and so are they. I do not have hard evidence of these facts, but if you do not do as I ask, and he and his people escape, you will be held accountable, as I am telling you he is deeply involved in this treacherous act against our country." Rawlings didn't say a word. He just looked at Willis and then agent Moore, who nodded her head in agreement. "I've already had your director appraised that you need more agents, right now, do just as Willis here has suggested," she said, "Put a man on him now- don't let him out of your sight," said Willis. But Pasha Yebnemko went nowhere. He stood in sight, processing the scene. Meanwhile, the news service carried the story of the 310 souls killed aboard flight 1504 and the sole survivor who landed the plane, an 11-year-old boy whose name was not being released.

* * * * * * * * *

Willis' father arrived, and it was show time. "Okay, everyone," said Willis, "It's showtime. Everyone, please be seated in the designated area so I can say this once and once only." Yebnemko sat in the last seat nearest the exit. Two officers stood behind him by the exits. "First of all, my father's here. If any attempt to take my life is made, he will thwart it because, like many of you, he is an expert marksman. I do not trust the powers that be; this is why I waited to tell my story because I was worried that someone might try to take my life here in order to stop me from uncovering a very nasty set of principles. My father will kill any of you who tries anything, so bear that in mind. The beautiful agent Moore would do the same, but because of her obvious beauty, I did not wish to jeopardize her. Yes, chivalry is not dead. Anyway, this is what happened: While on the plane I was in the galley area and saw three men approaching. The men at boarding time appeared relaxed and gave off the impression of being glad to be getting back home, but once the flight took off, their demeanor changed; they became brisker, more assertive, more aggressive, and being raised on and off military bases I recognized them for who they truly were, mercenaries, but gave no thought to them. Until they approached the galley area where I was, hidden in the pantry cabinet under the counter, playing around, and they convened right in front of me to finalize their hijacking scheme, and I heard the whole plan unbeknownst to them.

"They fanned out to assume positions. When d-time came, the man who stood in the pantry's beeper went off, signaling the onset of the deployment of poisonous gas. When he went to put his mask on, I partially stepped out of my hiding place, snatched his mask, and locked myself back in the pantry closet and put on the mask, as he tried to get in but failed, then was overcome by the fumes. After the fumes cleared, I came out and saw the second man heading my way. I put the mask back on the dead 'comrade' and went back into hiding. The man saw his comrade dead and thought it was due to a faulty mask. He had no idea there was someone still alive on board. After he went back up front, I decided to slink to one of the passengers, get their cell phone, and call for help; then I realized that the only one who could help me at 35,000 feet was me. At this point, the man was on his phone and headed back my way. I procured a weapon, two to be exact, this knife and this fire extinguisher, and hid in the bathroom stall this time. The man stopped in front of my stall, and I heard the gist of his conversation, and I heard a name." When I said this, I glanced at Pasha, but he didn't notice because he was busy looking at his fingernails. I continued: "Then the man went and used the stall next to me. I opened my stall door, stood up on the lip of the toilet seat, and when the man came out and walked by, I jumped all out and swung this fire extinguisher," (and held it up for everyone to see), "with all my might and bashed him on the side of the head. He went down, I hit him again, and he went out. I then used this knife," and held it up for all to see, "and snipped his spinal cord so he couldn't walk (something my father taught me); I then took his phone."

At this, Pasha looked up. Willis then took the phone out of his pocket, put it on the table, and slid it over to agent Moore. "It has the number the man called, plus a wealth of other stuff, too, probably." Agent Moore picked up the phone, and started going through it, opened her laptop, and really started to get into it. Willis got up and started walking slowly with the fire extinguisher in his hand and continued with what happened, "Then I ran straight to the cockpit and ran inside of it and bashed the last guy's head into submission, tied and gagged him, then snipped his spine too. While the plane was inbound, I tortured and beat the crap out of them, which explains the extent of their injuries. When the boarding party came in, one cop started frisking the two men who I had placed by the cockpit door, so I could keep an eye on them." Willis was directly behind Yebnemko now; he stopped, "then the frisking cop made a mistake. He asked me where the other man was. I never once said there were three hijackers over that radio, so how did this cop know that? Also, in the conversation, I overheard the man say, you're a police officer, 'Pasha,' and I knew instinctively that the frisking offer was one and the same, and that suspicion was confirmed when I found out that officer Yebnemko, here, whose first name is Pasha, and he's a Chech-Chen nationalist." Pasha Yebnemko put his hand on his sidearm and went to get up simultaneously, and Willis hit him with the fire extinguisher. He fell sideways, his gun clattering to the floor, and Willis hit him again, and he was out cold.

Yebnemko woke up cuffed to a chair, hands, and feet. After his vision cleared, he could see Willis clearly. Willis walked over to him and said, "See, I told you that you would get the fire extinguisher, just like your friends." Everyone in the room started laughing. From the information gathered off the phone and various raids, all the mercenaries involved were captured and charged for their duplicity in the crime and faced a barrage of other charges. Pasha and the two men would eventually receive the death penalty for their roles in the hijacking. Their plot was to extort one hundred million from the government in return for the Americans on board the plane. Even though American policy is not to negotiate with terrorists, it's a well-known fact that they do so under the table. In this case, after the money was wired to a Swiss bank account, the mercenaries never planned a safe return for the passengers; they planned to refuel the plane in New York and fly around in circles until they got confirmation of payment, then they would put the plane on autopilot headed straight for the empire state building and bail out with parachutes into the east river, where a boat with their comrades would pick them up as the plane was crashing into the empire state building. They would then let the media know and say the United States Government refused to pay, so their compatriots were killed. But it was a plan that would never come to fruition because of the intelligence and heart of an 11-year-old American boy.

THE TEENAGER

Willis Dash was smarter than the average boy his age. He was now 14 and just finished his second semester of college at U.S.C. He spoke six languages fluently, one of them being Russian, which is why he understood every word of the brief exchange between the two men who acted as though they had just met up, as planned, for lunch.

He was sitting with his books open at an outdoor cafe, studying nuclear biology, toying with a sandwich. All morning long, he'd been semi-distracted from his studying because he had an uneasy feeling and couldn't figure out what it was, but now he knew he was being watched.

The two men bro-hugged and spoke in their native tongue, not knowing that Willis understood every word. They separated, and one held the other by his shoulders, trying to make it seem to anyone who observed them that they hadn't seen each other in a while. They spoke in Russian.
"That's him, sitting there, with books open, reading," said the first.

"Fine, I'll take him when he leaves," said the other, laughing, trying to continue the deceit of two friends just meeting up.
"Uri and Anton are at the east end, and Vlad and Mikael at the west," said the first.
"Good, we will sit and eat and wait for our brother's enemy." Said the second.
"He must be taken alive," said the first.
"This I know, and so does everyone," said the second one. "We will follow him to his campus- it's very spacious- and take him there," said the first.

Willis looked around very carefully. He could detect no surveillance at either end of the street. He looked across the street at the rows of stores, assessing for his best course of action. He wouldn't go out the back; they'd have that covered. He knew that they'd have it covered once he entered one of the stores across the street. He knew he had to neutralize their numbers in order to escape. He was unarmed, except for his trusty Swiss army knife.

After another slow twenty minutes of waiting, hoping a cop car would come by, he decided to move; the cops were never around when you really needed them. He was no coward, but these men were big and obviously trained mercenaries. On the plane, he had the advantage of surprise; here it was not so. In fact, they thought they had the advantage of surprise, but they didn't, and that was his edge if any. He got up, folded his books up, put them in his book bag, and went into the cafe to the bathroom. One of them followed directly behind him. There were three urinals. Willis went to the third urinal, away from the door. The man came in and went first by the door. Willis stood like he was using it, then flushed, and then moved towards the opposite wall where the sinks were as if he was about to wash his hands, then spun very adroitly back towards the man whose back was towards him, legs spread as though he was urinating, and kicked upwards, catching him in the balls, he immediately fell to the floor doubled up in pain and Willis stomped on his head one time. The force slammed the man's head against the tiled floor rendering him unconscious. Willis took his wallet, looked at his phone, memorized the numbers, and then put the phone back, not wanting them to use the G.P.S. to track him if he did take it. He emerged from the bathroom and made a bee line across the street to a clothing store, never looking back.

Alexia Zadzap watched as Willis emerged, walked out and across the street, and spoke into his wrist mike, "Don't lose him," then went into the bathroom to see what was taking his partner so long. His partner lay flat on his back, unconscious, with a small pool of blood under his head. He checked him quickly, his phone he took but noticed his wallet was missing; he spoke into his wrist mike, "Burdov is down, I repeat down, do not let the subject get away." He decided he didn't care who saw; he'd take the boy wherever he caught him.

Willis entered the store and pulled out his phone, and confirmed what he already knew that it needed recharging. He could not get any of the innocent people in the store involved; to do so would ensure their deaths and their families because these men were ruthless killers. He grabbed some pants and went to the fitting room as though to try them on and went straight out the window while trying to figure out how they found him. It's been three years since the plane incident. Someone inside the government had to be involved; that's the only way they could have possibly found him or known his name. This also meant that his father and possibly his mother were also in jeopardy; he had to act fast, but first and foremost, he had to lose his pursuers.

He emerged in an alley behind the stores. As he neared the exit, he saw two men nonchalantly coming his way. They didn't see him. He turned back around and scampered to a delivery truck, a semi. He got up on the dock, then some crates, and climbed to the truck's top. He debated with himself briefly if he should lay on the roof of the truck and ride it out when it left but was unsure how long it would be before it left, so he decided to keep moving.

Atop the truck's roof, he jumped to the back awning of the store and from there he made his way to the roof, then went straight down till he reached the end and looked over cautiously. He spotted them. He stood stock still thinking. He knew what he'd do. He went to the second store from the end, a woman's boutique store. He deftly cut the alarm wire of the roof door with this Swiss army knife and entered. Once downstairs he grabbed a print dress, a fake bosomed bra, sandals, and an oversized straw hat, sunglasses, and a large shoulder bag... slipped into the ladies' room and changed into them. When he emerged, he was a sight to see. He went to the counter, paid for his goods, and then left the store.

He walked nonchalantly as though shopping, stopping for minutes at a time, looking in windows like a true consumer, all the while looking for the placement of his pursuers. He spotted four men on foot and another four in two separate cars stationed at opposite ends of the street. Of the four men on foot, two were on each side of the streets checking stores, working individually. Willis correctly assumed that while these men were ruthless mercenaries, they were not well versed in the art of cloak and dagger, and neither was he, but he felt instinctively that he held the advantage, and while he had it, he must keep it in order to stay alive.

As he was walking, one of the men came straight toward Willis. Willis was walking with arms folded, pushing the fake bosoms up a Little. He had his Swiss army knife in his right hand under his left bicep. As the man neared, he looked at the fake tits, then at Willis' sun-glassed face, and smiled. Willis smiled back. The man then turned and went into the store. Willis went right in behind him. The man looked around carefully and not spotting Willis, went towards the bathroom Willis walked right behind him. The man pushed open the bathroom door slowly, peered in cautiously, and was just about to enter when Willis stabbed him in the base of his neck, hitting the spinal cord and severing it. The man crumpled like an old accordion and hit the ground face-first, knocking out his two front teeth and then he started choking to death because his head's angle was blocking his breathing. Willis straightened his head, keeping him. Alive, took his wallet and his gun to use, if necessary, but mainly he wanted it for prints. Then decided to make sure he got prints. He emptied the wallet in his bag, pressed the man's fingers firmly on the leather of the wallet, and then put that in his bag. Carefully he dragged him further into the bathroom and then left.

"Boris, do you read me?" Alexia Zadzap asked, receiving no answer from his hails; he pulled out his phone and locked it onto Boris' G.P.S., which indicated the store he was in. He then hailed Marchenko.
"Marchenko here."
"Boris is not responding. He's four stores in front of you; see to him, now," said the Commander Zadzap.
"Yes, Sir!" replied Marchenko.

Willis waited, knowing the other agent would arrive shortly. He stood at a counter almost to the rear of the store apparently examining makeup items. The man named

Marchenko entered the store cautiously. He reminded Willis of a big cat he'd seen on the discovery channel. He was cautious and extremely dangerous. He came toward Willis on his way to the bathroom. When he came near enough, Willis turned to him and said: "Excuse me, would you like it if your lady wore this perfume?" and pushed the bottle towards Marchenko. Marchenko sidestepped Willis and said, "I'm not interested, whore." Then Willis sprayed the perfume in his eyes. He brought both hands up to shielding his eyes and Willis stabbed him in his heart and killed him instantly. Marchenko fell backward, toppling over a rack of clothing. People started turning around, wondering what was going on. Willis bent over him, took his wallet and gun and prints, and said over his shoulder, "someone call an Ambulance- I think this man is having a heart attack." Got up and left.

When Willis got out front, he could hear the piercing screams of the approaching police sirens. Apparently, someone had found the first guy and called the cops. Commotions were going on from both sides of the streets. People were making it harder for the men to find him; he noticed that at the end of the block, the surveillance car only held one man now. He headed that way. He came to a vegetable stand, stopped-bought a huge watermelon, then proceeded toward the car where the lone man sat, waiting for his comrades. When Willis got to about 5" in front of the car, he slid the gun he'd taken from the man out of the shoulder bag, jammed the barrel deeply in the side of the watermelon, facing the driver, and as he walked directly by the car door, he pulled the trigger. The watermelon did just what Willis knew it would, silence the shot; it muted it perfectly. The man's head exploded in a pink mist, and the watermelon fell to pieces by the car's back door almost an instant later. Willis kept on going as though nothing had happened. No one reacted in any kind of way until Willis was about half a block away. He heard a scream and glanced back to see a woman pointing in the car, acting hysterical at the gory sight. A police car pulled up, and Willis got away from there, unobserved by them.

Alexia Zadzap and the remainder of his team were livid. Totally and completely angry and incensed that not only did a 14-year-old schoolboy elude and evade capture, but he also incapacitated three of his men in the process. But the worst part of it was that he couldn't get a visual on the kid; it was like he was invisible. Obviously, he had some kind of training, he thought to himself. His commander was not going to like this at all. About six blocks away, Willis found an internet cafe, recharged his phone, called his father, and gave him a brief outline of what had just happened. He, in turn, would check on his mother and have security alerted to the threat. Willis called the station chief of Homeland Security to ascertain where the beautiful Special Agent Katheryn Moore was.

"Homeland Security, how may I help you?" asked a ruff voice.
"Patch me through to Special Agent Moore, please," he said.
"Please state the nature of your business, sir," said the voice.
"It's a highly personal matter which I cannot disclose to you over the phone," said Willis.
"Do you have a credible issue for Agent Moore?" he asked.
"Yes, tell her it's 11 W.D. on the line, and if you don't, your ass is mine, and you'll not be answering any more phones for any department of the state," said Willis.
"Please hold while I connect you, sir," said the man in a shocked tone. On his desk was a memo with a list of names that were to be processed immediately, and 11 W.D. was one of them. The memo had been on his

desk for 3 years now and it had been updated several times and always, that name remained at the top of the list. Something big must be going on, he thought as he rerouted the call.

"Special Agent Moore speaking, please identify yourself and the nature of your business," she said in a sweet but guarded voice.

"11 W.D., a.k.a. fire extinguisher," said Willis. Katheryn Moore immediately recognized the voice and felt the sincerity with which he spoke to her. Being that he used his code name, so would she.

"Hello, 11, how've you been?" she said.

"Missing you," he said it so slowly and tenderly that she immediately felt a wave of love surge through her and wanted to see him immediately.

"I want to see you right now," she said."Good. I need to see you too. I also need an emergency evac," he said. When she heard of an emergency evac, she became very concerned.

"What's the problem, and where are you?" She asked.

"San Diego," he said. "Some men tried to kill me."

"Go to the naval station. Ask for Admiral Decker; he'll be expecting you," she said.

* * * * * * * * *

Rear Admiral Stanton Decker sat behind his desk reading a file and gestured for Willis to sit and continued reading as if Willis wasn't there; Willis didn't like it. He looked around the decorated office, trying to locate the hidden camera because his mind told him there was one somewhere, along with a listening device. Admiral Decker started without speaking without preamble.

"Knew your father, you know."

"How long before my flight is ready?" asked Willis.

"You want to tell me what's this all about?" he asked, not answering Willis.

"National Security mines and my family," said Willis.

"I read your file," he said and pushed the file he was reading toward Willis, whose curiosity got the best of him. He reached for the file and started skimming through it.

"Got anything to do with what's in that file?" He asked.

"Yes," said Willis not looking up.

"What's in the diplomatic pouch?" asked Admiral Decker.

"Lunch," replied Willis, not Looking up and continuing to read the file.

"May I join you?" he asked.

"No." said Willis.

"Why?" he asked.

"I'm dining with Agent Moore," replied Willis.

"As soon as a hard copy file is made, I'll Know," he said.

"So will anyone who has the money to pay for it," replied Willis.

"Do you really believe that?" He asked.

"I believe that to be a fact, the greed of Americans will be our downfall one day," replied Willis.

"If you have proof or suspicions of such nefarious acts, please point me in the right direction, and I will act accordingly," he said.

"I'll handle it myself." Said Willis.

"If you need anything, give me a call," he said.

"Copy that," replied Willis.

****

Under different circumstances, Willis would have liked to look around and see what Kansas was all about; he thought to himself as he looked down from the windshield of the all-black jet ranger helicopter at the heartland. Beneath him, he could see miles and miles of open grassland sprouting wheat that fed not only America but people all over the world. The Homeland Security facility was located about 20 miles outside of Kansas City. It was a beautiful state-of-the-art facility situated in the nest of some foothills. But just like an iceberg, 75 percent of it was underground. It was a massive complex and resembled a garrison more than anything else. It held everything an intelligence agency could possibly want. It even had its own dog unit.

Willis was ushered to an underground command center that was huge. It had workstations and video monitors all over the place. At the far end, a huge video screen stood; the largest in the room, with smaller ones at the sides of it, was alive with real-time satellite or drone footage in the progress of a raid somewhere in the middle east. Special Agent Katheryn Moore and several others stood Looking at the monitor with rapt attention. When the words "Prisoner is secured, all hostages safe," came across the intercom, a loud resounding cheer rippled throughout the room. Hugs and handshaking ensued, and amid all the glee, Katheryn Moore glimpsed Willis standing there smiling at her. She came straight to him and hugged him fiercely. "Everyone quiet down for a second," she said, "I want you all to meet a V.I.P. He is to be accorded anything he needs without hesitation; this is Captain Dwayne Dash, U.S.A.F.'s son Willis."

"That's him!" Someone said, "The kid who landed the plane in New York!" And everyone in the place left their stations and came over to him, shook his hand, and patted him on the back with congratulations of all kinds. While it was all very flattering, someone in this room could be selling secrets, like his name.

* * * * * * * * *

Alexia Zadzap and the rest of his team headed east by car to Arizona, where they would receive intel on where to pick up the boy. They were also told that failure was not an option. If they couldn't accomplish the mission, they might as well pick a cemetery they wanted to be interred in. Their commander was overwhelmed with rage at what had happened thus far. The boy was responsible for foiling their hijacking plot to raise the money they needed to fund their war against the Russian government. He's now killed three, paralyzed three, and the seventh one, who begged for the assignment because one of the agents that were killed was his first cousin, now lay in a coma in a San Diego hospital. The only good thing was he couldn't be charged with a major felony because he committed no crime except entering America illegally if they found out who he was, and they probably would. But none of that made one wit of a difference if he didn't wake up out of the coma. Alexia himself just wanted to kill the kid. His commander wanted him captured so he could torture and then kill him. Alexia didn't like being made a fool of; he was determined not to let it happen again. He would kill the boy on sight by accident and deal with his commander later there would be no getting away this time.

* * * * * * * *

"You've grown so big, Willis," said Agent Moore as they entered her office, "the last time I saw you, you were 4' 2," now look at you, you're the same height as me, and I'm 5' 6.""
"Yes, and I'm still a virgin," said Willis smiling.
"That's obviously by choice," she said smiling right back.
"Yes, I'm saving myself for you," he responded, still smiling.
"Maybe when you're 21," she said.
"Try 18," he said, and she giggled.
"Maybe, now tell me what happened," and he did. When he finished, she turned on her laptop, and a big video screen on the wall came on. She then accessed the cameras

along the street, and he pointed out the men, and she targeted their faces for facial recognition. He opened the pouch and gingerly gave her the wallet to have it dusted for prints. He decided to keep the gun.
"You have access to satellite imagery, don't you?" he asked. "Of course," she answered.
"May I see some of the areas in question?" He asked. She looked at him hard for a minute before speaking, "Yes, you may." Then she tapped out some commands on her laptop, and then San Diego appeared. She showed him how to operate the software and left him alone as she went to get the wallet dusted for prints and use the bathroom.

Willis rewound the footage and then zoomed in. He watched as the men initially came and sat at the cafe table next to him. He rewound it slowly to when they first entered the area, watched himself appear on the roof, fast-forwarding it to when he left and watched as the remaining men got into their car and went east. He continued watching until he got an angle good enough to get the car's plate number and model and jotted it down. He sped up the footage and watched as the car entered Arizona, then watched as they entered a yard. He took down the address. He fast-forwarded it, watched them leave, and followed their progress to a house approximately 100 miles south of where he now stood. Then one man came out, got in the car, and left. He kept watching the house. A while later, a different car pulled up and went inside. Willis correctly assumed that they had ditched the first car. Katheryn Moore came back, and he asked her to get I.C.E. to search the house for illegal immigrants, but what I really wanted to get were computers or phones. She said she would try, but as the men had broken no laws there was no probable cause to search their residence. The computer pinged and Katheryn Moore opened the facial recognition software app and there they were. The men of the surveillance team who wanted him dead. All Ukraine Nationals and Chechen rebels, all with seemingly legal entry documents. "You need to find out who issued those visas; he or she is probably a mole," said Willis; she got up and left to do just that.

Willis left her office and went looking for, and found, the motor pool. The officer in charge asked Willis for his autograph. Willis asked for a motorcycle to check the surrounding area to kill some time. The man gave him a lime green Kawasaki 225. Willis tightened the nap sack on his back, put on the helmet, and tore ass out of there doing a wheelie for half a mile down the straight away from the compound. He headed straight south for the house where the men were. Time was of the essence. Doing the speed limit, he would get there in a little over an hour, but he wouldn't be doing it; he would just have to risk it. He couldn't let them get away. He felt sure the men would be heading for New York; he was determined that they wouldn't get that far.

Special Agent Katheryn Moore came back to her office to find Willis gone. She put out a page for him, then went to her laptop and activated her snoop program, which recorded the strokes of the previous user. She soon was viewing what Willis had viewed. When her page was answered by the motor pool informing her that Willis was mobile and out joy riding, she bought the satellite view of the compound online and rewound it until she picked up Willis and saw him heading due south at top speed and knew exactly where he was headed, they didn't call her Special Agent E.S.P. for nothing. She burst out of her office, grabbed seven agents, went straight to the motor pool, got cars, and went after Willis.

About halfway to his destination, Willis spotted a mom-and-pop hardware store in a small village on the route he was taking. He slowed down, made a U-turn, pulled up out front, got off the bike, and went in. He bought a razor-sharp bowie knife, duct tape, a can of raid, a lighter, and a small pair of binoculars, then headed out.

Katheryn Moore, from the back seat of the suburban, watched Willis from her laptop satellite link and wondered what he was up to when he stopped and entered the store. She knew, as a professional, that she was taking too much liberty with Willis. He'd already killed several men, albeit in self-defense, and yet she felt no urge whatsoever as an officer of the law to bring him in. She knew she wouldn't, she liked him, plain and simple, and she knew he'd already been through a lot and felt the dark forces of other men's minds had ultimately led him to do what he did and what he was about to do now. She just wanted him to channel his superior intellect into something more rewarding than becoming a potential serial killer because if he did, there was no way anyone would catch him; he was just too smart. She knew what she would do. She would ask his father to nudge him toward the C.I.A. based on the training that would solidify his mind into righteousness for his country, which he obviously loves, lest he go off the deep end, and also, he could still fly planes, which is what he loves most. Even though he was 14, she could get him clearance to enter at 16, but would he be receptive to the idea? She would run it by his father as soon as she got back and see what he thought.

Her laptop pinged, and she split-screened it to respond to the hail while keeping an eye on Willis. It was a bulletin from the San Diego Branch of Homeland Security, notifying them of the deaths of the Ukrains, who were believed, illegal aliens, and did Homeland have any interest in them, and whether they could provide intel on the potential killer, who was a person of interest, a female approximately 20 to 30 years old, 5' 5" and showed a sketchy grainy photo. The face couldn't be made out at all, but she knew it was Willis, as he had already told her what and how he had done it, and she giggled at the picture and thought to herself that they'd never find him.

* * * * * * * * *

Alexia Zadzap liked America for some reason. It wasn't like the way people made it out to be. Americans had freedoms. They lived not in fear. They did as they pleased, unaware of the foulness of their government, or maybe they just didn't care. He wished his people were able to live so. But for the most part, the Russian government was too controlling. They had to be made aware that they should treat their people better; that is why his homeland of Chechnya wouldn't submit and would fight to the end. We would have been better off if it weren't for the boy. The boy was an aberration. Surely all boys of America couldn't be like him cause if they were, they most certainly wouldn't be able to conquer America, not that they'd want to. The boy had killed and maimed several of his countrymen, so he must pay.

He received a phone call and left the men at the house to go to the post office to pick up a priority mail pouch which discloses the latest intel on the boy's location and that of his parents. If they couldn't get him, they'd get them. Willis watched Alexia Zadzap get in the car and leave by himself. That made one less man to deal with. He would have to act fast because he didn't know how long he would be gone. He decided to kill the three in the house outright and wait for the other one to come, and he would torture him for the information he sought. He slipped up to the house after stashing the bike. He pulled out the gun he'd kept and put the bowie knife in his waist. He looked through the window to locate the men. Two were sitting in the living room talking, and the third he couldn't Locate. He must be in the bathroom or on the second floor somewhere. Willis was in a semi-crouched stance and was about to step back away from the window when a hand grabbed his right shoulder and spun him around violently. Willis went with the spin, using it to swing back fast with the gun extended. The barrel clipped the man on his right temple with a solid thud, the man's grip loosened, and Willis swung the gun again back the other way, catching him flush on the jaw, and he went down and landed flat on his back. Willis jumped on him again, whacked him twice on the head, rolled him over, pulled out the bowie knife, and pushed it into the base of the man's neck, paralyzing him instantly, and to make sure he didn't wake up and yell out. He yanked his head back and slit his throat from ear to ear. Blood started gushing out like a broken water main. He wiped the blade off the man's shirt and dragged him from the back of the house out of the line of sight from the house. He then walked up to the porch and entered the house like he lived there, his gun extended. He walked through the kitchen through a small hallway right into the living room where the two remaining men sat and sat right across from them and didn't say a word, just held the gun on his lap, pointing at them. One of the men glanced toward the back, and Willis said, "Your friend won't be coming back to help you." They spoke to each other in Russian and said, "If we both charge him, he can only get one of us."

"Let your conscience be your guide," said Willis in Russian; both men were stunned and looked at each other then one of them spoke; "You are Russian; they told us you were American."

"I am American, true blue," stated Willis flatly.

"So how can your Russian be so flawless?" asked one.

"I taught myself. Once I grasped your barbaric undertones, it was easy," responded Willis disrespectfully.

"What now, then?" said the second one.

"Who are you getting your information from about my whereabouts?" asked Willis.

"That's something you'll never know," said the first.

"You'd rather die?" asked Willis.

"For our cause and country, yes," said the second, and Willis shot him in the kneecap, it burst open with the boom sending flesh, blood, and cartilage on over the place and Both men. He screamed out in pain and fell to the floor; grabbing his knee, the other man reached for his gun, and just as it cleared his waist, Willis shot him between the eyes. He flew back onto the couch limp. He looked at the other man, who was rolling back and forth on the floor, holding his knee and moaning like the gunshot victim he was. "You can still live, you know, all you have to do is talk," said Willis.

"You'll kill me anyway if I do just like you did my comrades," he said painfully, rolling this way and that and holding his bloody knee moaning.

"No, if you talk, I'll leave you to get out of here the best what you know how," said Willis.

"I don't believe you," he said, moaning fiercely.

"Your buddy will be coming back soon- he can help you- just tell me who is giving you the information and I'll spare you," said Willis.

"Never!" He yelled.

"Have it your way," said Willis and shot him in the head.

* * * * * * * * *

Special Agent Katheryn Moore's convoy sped forward relentlessly. She watched as the satellite imagery became gray from cloud coverage, then completely unviewable. "Darn it," she thought to herself. It was okay because she knew exactly where Willis was going. As the convoy sped along, they came to a rise and went over it; they could see at its base a freight train as it rolled through. They stopped at the crossing and had to wait and watch as railroad car after the car took its sweet time going by.

* * * * * * * * *

Alexia Zadzap was in good spirits despite his previous failure. He was in good spirits because of the priority mail pouch he just received from his contact in Washington. He was to go to New York to get the boy's mother, who had been moved to the air force base in Plattsburgh. Once she left the base, she would be taken. But first, he had to go to the safe house in Brighton Beach, Brooklyn.

As he pulled up to the house, he was preoccupied with thoughts of New York. He had been there before; some of the eating houses were excellent, especially in what they called midtown. He also loved the theaters.

Broadway was far better at exhibiting live stage shows than anywhere he had ever been, and he couldn't wait to take one in. He liked classical music, and Carnegie Hall was alive with great symphonies nightly. Yes, he would enjoy New York while awaiting the green light to go to Plattsburgh. He
knew it might be a long wait as they had to let the last event die down slowly.

Alexia Zadzap stepped through the screen door into the small hallway to the living room and stopped at the entrance, stunned. His two comrades lay dead, surrounded by pools of blood. He started backing away, unwilling to investigate further, when a momentary flash of pain crossed his mind, then nothing as he fell unconscious. Willis duct taped his mouth, hands, and feet, dragged him out to his own car, wrestled his body into the trunk, retrieved the priority mail pouch, got in the car, and drove away.

* * * * * * * * *

After a twenty-minute wait, the convoy finally was underway again and reached the house forty-five minutes later. They jumped out of their Suburban's brandishing guns, and two went to each side of the house, making their way to the back; the remainder went to the front door, which stood wide open. They found the grizzly scene eerie, and each shuddered a little at the loss of life. The agents outside found the other man dead out back of the house. Special Agent Katheryn Moore told her men to search the place and report back to her. She went to her suburban and opened her laptop and started tapping away. All the while worrying about Willis because the car the men drove was missing. That could mean several things. Either someone got away, or that someone got Willis or Willis got him. Finding the car was paramount. She bought the recorded satellite footage that Willis was viewing, zoomed in on the last car to enter the place, got its specks, called the local police force and state troopers, and issued a federal A.P.B. for the car. She notified the locals of the dead men and requested that they secure the scene but not process it as a matter of national security. The reason for that was simple. She wanted to make sure Willis wouldn't be identified through D.N.A. samples; although she was sure he wouldn't be careless, it was nothing for a strand of hair to fall loose during an encounter and place a person at a scene. She didn't have to worry about the local's false claims of national security because one of her agents reported that they had found illegally altered automatics weapons, R.P.G.'s, grenades for such, and counterfeiting machine along with counterfeit bills in excess of a hundred thousand dollars in the basement. She waited till the F.B.I. arrived, briefed them, and left with her team to help scour the area for the car.

* * * * * * * * *

Willis drove about three miles away into a deeply wooded area and got to work. First, he duct-taped the Russian thoroughly to a tree. Then he drove the car into a ravine and covered it completely with branches and shrubbery. He then jogged back to where he had stashed the bike, and as he was about to rev it up, saw the Homeland Security convoy sped by on its way to the house. He was sure Ms. Moore was with them because she was the only smart one; she was the only one with the brains to figure it out. Besides his parents, she was the only person with whom he could have a conversation that wasn't lopsided. He revved up and went to take care of business. This situation needed closure, and he intended to get it.

Willis sat in front of Alexia Zadzap lotus style, reading the coded Letter from the priority mail pouch. He glanced at several pictures of his mother, which incensed him with rage, but he had to keep his cool.

"This is my mother, and what does this letter say?" asked Willis, although he already knew. He asked to judge the man's temperament. loosened the gag, and the man started chattering away in Russian, saying he didn't understand English, which Willis knew was a lie.

"That's okay, I speak Russian," the man was stunned. That's how I knew you were after me in San Diego when your buddy, who I killed, as you know, walked up and pointed me out to you."

"You are Russian?" he asked.

"No-American, do you want to live to fight another day?" asked Willis.

"Who doesn't want to live or die for his country?" asked the man.

"As it stands now, the police have nothing on you, are not looking for you, so if I let you go, you can go home," said Willis.

"But you will not let me go home," he said.

"Yes, I will. I have nothing against you; you have something against me. You want to kill me because I killed your comrades, but I didn't kill your comrades for no other reason than self-defense. Even on the plane, I just wanted to live. Is that so hard to understand?" asked Willis.

"No, it is not, but I do not have the information you seek."

"Tell me what this coded letter says about my family," said Willis although he already knew.

"Nothing, just the name, and address," he stated.

"See, you are lying, I'm trying to work with you, give you a chance, and you're lying. I already decoded it," said Willis.

"Really?" he said.

"It says the name, address and that my mother moved to Plattsburgh air force base and that you're to go to New York and remain there until you're notified to move on the subject," Alexia was amazed. This kid must be some kind of genius.

"Okay, I lied. I lied because I do not believe you will let me live."

"I only kill when I am forced to. You will live this day, but I will harm you irreparably if you do not tell me what I want to know."

"Like how?" asked Alexia. Willis pulled out the can of raid and the lighter, and the bowie.

"Feeling these?" he asked. Alexia looked hard at the items, not knowing their significance but not wanting to find out either so he said nothing.

"I'm just following orders," said Alexia.

"I understand that. Just tell me who here in Washington is giving you the intel." said Willis.

"I do not know his name; I just call a number and go to the nearest post office and pick up the coded message," Willis pulled out Alexias' phone and checked the phone list; which number?" he asked Alexia- told him. Willis would have then all checked anyway.

"Let me tell you something about me," started Willis, "I'm a behavioral scientist expert, and I know when someone's lying to me, and right now, you're lying to me. What's your contact's name- last chance, Alexia," said Willis firmly.

"I told you— I don't know," he said.

"Okay, have it your way," said Willis, "I'll start lightly, and if you continue to lie, it will get progressively worse." Then he gagged him, grabbed his left ear, and sliced it clean off with the razor-sharp bowie. Alexia screamed into his gag as loud as he could. He tried to move this way and that but was subdued by the tape. Willis could see the pain in his eyes. He cut off a piece of Alexia's shirt, balled it up, and taped it over his ear. "See, I studied a medical dictionary once, which is how I know to staunch the wound. isn't that nice of me, Alexia?" asked Willis, removing the gag. "I asked you a question Alexia," said Willis. "Yes, it was nice of you," he replied. "Good," said Willis, "Now we're getting somewhere. I really don't want to hurt you, Alexia. Don't think I do, but I need your contact's name. I must protect my family, Alexia. So, I ask you again, what is your contact's name?" Alexia was moaning in pain. He looked up and said, "I- I don't know his name, I swear to you." Willis didn't let him finish; he gagged him again, took off his shoes and socks, and pulled out the can of raid and the lighter. "Apparently, you have toe jam, so I'm going to help you get rid of it, permanently," he said and sprayed the roach spray over Alexias feet, then sat on Alexias legs with his back toward his face so his body weight would stop him from moving his legs, took the raid can, aimed it at Alexias feet, sprayed his toes again and sparked the lighter in front of the spray. It ignited and started burning Alexia's toes. Alexia started screaming through the gag and moving fiercely, trying to move his feet from in front of the flames, but it didn't work; then his thrashing and screaming stopped, and Willis stopped and looked back at Alexia- he passed out. Willis got up, turned around, and slapped the shit out of him, reviving him. The burning flesh stank horribly. Willis took off his gag and told him, "From this, you can recover, but from what I am about to do next, you'll hate me for life. If you do not tell me what I want to know now, I'm going to burn your eyes out, then burn your dick off. The choice is yours if you want to live without both. You'll no longer be good to your cause; who's your contact?" And held the can and lighter in front of his face, and he said, "Okay, I'll tell you."

* * * * * * * * *

They could find no trace of the car or Willis. Special Agent Katheryn Moore was worried. She did not want to call his father with the news of Willis' disappearance. She decided to wait a little longer and hoped that he would turn up soon. When they pulled up in front of the compound, a rush of relief washed over her when she saw the motorcycle parked out front against a rail. She hurried up inside to look for him and found him inside her office eating a sandwich.
"Hello, beautiful, looking for me?" he asked smiling.
"Willis, you cannot go around dispensing justice as you see fit," she said very concernedly, and he noticed.
"I wasn't dispensing justice, as you put it; I was merely on a fact-finding mission to persuade the parties involved to be

forthcoming as they were apprehensive about being so," she giggled.

"Willis, I am very worried about you. You've been through a very harrowing situation, and now this. I don't want you to go over the deep end and end up on the wrong side of the fence, physically as well as mentally, that's all. Is that too much to ask? Plus, you're putting me in the line of fire as I not only know of your undertakings, but I'm keeping quiet about it, and if my bosses found out, I'd be in trouble."

"I apologize for not being considerate of your position; it won't happen again. I felt the need to act was essential as the opportunity was golden and I don't have any restrictive guidelines to follow in pursuing constructive intel."

"You could've been hurt, Willis," she said with genuine concern.

"Of course, you're right, and I apologize for my actions," he said sincerely. They stood still, just staring at each other silently, for a few minutes then Willis said, "I've gained some valuable intel, and passed her the phone he'd taken from Alexia.

"Research those numbers and act on the info pronto. Once they realize their man is
down, they'll change everything, so you need to act fast. Several cells are plotting nefarious acts to raise money to fund their cause." She

took the phone and left and returned about fifteen minutes later.

"Willis, there's something I want you to do for me," she said.

"Which is?" he asked.

"When you turn 16, I can get you into the C.I.A., whichever branch you want. You can learn to fly whatever military craft you want and do all types of clandestine operations. They need smart people like you. I can see you eventually being the director there because your intellect knows no boundaries. You were born to make a difference, Willis, and in that department, you would be unfettered to do so."

"Actually, I wouldn't mind doing just that, Ms. Moore, because I don't fit in the regular force, and I don't want to be in the air force anymore either because their rules of engagement are a wee bit too pedestrian for my needs."

"So, you'll do it?" she asked.

"I think so, but in the meantime, do you know the Russian attaché to their embassy, Boris Gorbachov?" he asked.

"No, I don't know him, but I've seen him around in D.C. once or twice, why?" she asked guardedly.

"He's the one who gave the mercenaries my name and family's address. I need to find out who gave him the info, who's on his payroll," said Willis.

"Willis, he has diplomatic immunity," she replied.

"I'm not very diplomatic when it comes to my family's safety," he replied.

"Willis, you can't go after him," she said pleadingly. "You'll start a war."

"I'm not; I want his source. It must be a senator or a general with access to defense department files. All I want you to do is investigate his expenditures; I'll do rest," he said.

* * * * * * * * *

Willis did not like Special Agent Thomas Rawlings of the F.B.I. He'd first met him at the plane incident in New York and took an instant dislike to him because it was plain as day he was highly interested in Katheryn Moore, who Willis was also taken aback by. It was a case of two men wanting the same woman. Agent Rawlings only saw Katheryn Moore; he had no idea Willis liked her too and dismissed him outright as a little boy, making Willis even angrier.

The F.B.I. had been handed the task of finding out who was committing the treasonous act of selling state secrets to the Russians. It had been four months now with no progress being made and this along with Willis' natural dislike for agent Rawlings was making Willis very angry. He wanted results.

"Did I not tell you information was coming out of senator Brian McColloughs' office?" stated Willis angrily.
"First and foremost, we have not been able to get anything on him that would justify a warrant to delve further into his affairs. Secondly, I think your source might have given you a red herring," said Rawlings.
"First and foremost, the man is a United states senator and, as such, would have access to the intimate workings of the F.B.I. and would take measures to circumvent its techniques to avoid detection. Secondly, the only red herring I received was that you had the competency to get the job done," said Willis, seething.

    For the first time since meeting Willis, Special Agent Thomas Rawlings took a good look at Willis as an adversary. He considered that at 11 years old, he outsmarted and physically subdued three Russian mercenaries. He locked eyes with Willis and blinked first and thought to himself that Willis might be a little deranged, which was a serious miscalculation on his part. Physically he wasn't that little kid anymore; he was 14 now, 5' 6," which meant that he was not finished growing. His father was 6' 2" and a dangerous man and realized with a start that Willis was dangerous, not deranged. With that thought, he decided to take a different tact.

"How do you think you think we should proceed?" asked Rawlings.

"Have someone slip into the Russian attaché's secretaries house and plant ten pounds of heroin, then call the cops for a raid, then offer him a deal if he cooperates and tells us anything interesting. If he doesn't cooperate, we'll have the charges dropped because of unlawful search and seizure," said Willis.

"The Federal Bureau of Investigation doesn't operate in such an unlawful manner," said Rawlings.

"That's why other countries call the F.B.I. the Federal Bureau of Idiots," said Willis.

"Integrity is a blessing," said Rawlings.

"So is inane-ness, especially when it's in your anus," said Willis heatedly.

"Stop right there," said Katheryn Moore.

"I haven't even started yet," said Willis.

"Well, don't," she replied. Both Willis and Rawlings stood staring at each other. Several others in the room were giggling at the exchange. Rawlings boss, Brian Denton, intervened. "You two relax; it will take time to sort this out. The parties involved are vigilant in concealing the treason which Willis believes is taking place. The defense department has green-lighted the continued surveillance and will provide additional manpower to help. So, in the meantime, everyone stays focused on the objective."

* * * * * * * * *

Willis had been watching the Russian attaché's aide for a month now when he finally figured out how the communication lines were being operated. The attaché's aide, who was an American born of European parents, was the gopher. He was an openly gay man who frequented clubs of that nature. He would meet Senator McCollough's aide there, where the communications were passed on. This meant two things to Willis, not only was he passing information to the Russians, but he was also passing information to the Chechen rebels. He was a double agent, in America, with diplomatic immunity. He must feel pretty smug, thought Willis and started to figure out a way to get him back without starting a war with the two countries.

Willis wondered what it would take to get senator McCollough to come clean and wondered why the F.B.I. couldn't pick up the money trail because, surely, he wasn't doing it for free. Then it dawned on Willis that maybe the senator didn't know. Maybe someone else was stealing the information right out under his nose. It wouldn't be the first time something of this magnitude had happened. The information may not be coming from Senator McCollough at all, but another one who's paying McCollough's aide to be the messenger. The solution was McCollough's aide Mike Bastion.

* * * * * * * * *

Mike Bastion thought he was doing well for himself. His Cayman Island bank account now held close to two million dollars. Not bad, he thought, for three years' worth of work. He planned to retire soon. But he had to do it in a way that wouldn't get the Russians angry and wanting to kill him for what he knew or could say. In this respect, he was very naive, for as soon as he was deemed expendable, he would be killed to tie up a potential loose end. Mike knew that he shouldn't be spying on his own country, and he knew that treason was punishable by death, but he felt like America was going to the highest bidder anyway; seats in the senate and congress were routinely bought by lobbyists who put in their pawns to their bidding of self-interests and that of their groups. What he was doing was no different, he just did it in another way. He had made more money than ever without the limelight and prestige, which was fine with him. He wasn't an out in the open type of person anyway, which is how this whole thing got started in the first place.

Willis watched as Mike Bastion got in his car and drove off to work. He watched Mike's progress on his laptop- he had placed a G.P.S. indicator on the inside of the left front wheel well of mikes car so he could watch and record his movements in real-time. Willis snapped his laptop shut, went to the side of the door of Mike's house, picked the lock deftly, and entered. He walked around with his backpack on and his laptop open, watching to make sure Mike didn't double back. He found what he was looking for in the den, His P.C. He booted it up and quickly bypassed Mike's password. Mike was obviously computer-savvy. But after perusing his files for a half hour, Willis found nothing until he found a security monitor for the basement, which was triggered by motion sensors and once triggered, sounded alarms on Mike's phone and started recording with a live feed to Mikes phone. Willis disabled it and went to the basement to see what secrets it held, for he wasn't guarding that basement for nothing.

It took Willis ten minutes to locate the hidden motion sensors; they were in the boiler room, so whatever he was hiding was in there. The boiler room appeared to be concrete, and Willis started checking it for hidden compartments. He went around the tiny room but could detect no hidden compartment. He checked the ceiling, nothing. He checked the boiler, nothing. There was an old rusty air conditioning unit in one corner, upside down on the floor. He looked at it carefully and knew he'd found what he was looking for. Even though the A.C. was old and rusty, the screws in the back were bright and shiny and new. He dug into his backpack, pulled out a screwdriver, and opened the A.C. Inside, taped to one side firmly and neatly, were ten flash drives. He undid the taping with neat precision, removed the flash drives, copied them on his laptop, and then replaced them just as neatly as they were. He even had Elmer's glue in his pack, and he used this to reglue the tape, so it didn't come off after he left, which would indicate tampering with if Mike sees it.

He then packed up his stuff, returned upstairs, reactivated the security set up for the basement, and got out of there.

Once Willis got to his hotel, it took him no more than fifteen minutes to override the password and access the drive, and when he did, he said to himself, this dude was a fool to have such sensitive top security stolen files on record in his house and how he did it. He even had taped conversations with the Russian double agent Boris Gorbachov on how and when to make drops and negotiations on payment. The fool really thought he was a super spy. He now knew that Senator McCullough was not involved. Mike Bastion had installed a motion sensor camera and microphone into
the wall, the size of a pinhead, which was given to him by the Russians. It had a zoom camera, and its clarity was unbelievable. Whenever the senator entered his office and got on his computer, his every stroke was recorded, and so was every document on the screen. From there, it was just a matter of the price Mike wanted for what was on the screen. Mike's espionage dated back 3 years. Willis leaned back and thought long and hard about his next course of action. He wanted to Kill the Russian, his attaché, and most of all, Mike Bastion.

Willis requested a meeting with the director of Homeland Security and the F.B.I. and got it. A few other notables were there also, and agent Rawlings. Willis outlined what he did and showed them the copied discs. They sat there stunned. Willis continued: "As ambassador, Gorbachov is technically not prosecutable, but he must be expelled from our country for his role as a handler of his attaché and Mike Bastion. A top-secret investigation should be launched by the F.B.I. immediately, and photos taken of Bastion passing off the data and of the data being passed on to Gorbachov by his aide; Gorbachov must be caught with the goods red handed to ensure viable expulsion and international embarrassment. The attaché, Marcus Milanovic, and the senator's aide, Mike Bastion, should be given the death penalty. I'd like to kill them outright, but it would not be feasible to solidify the expulsion of Gorbachov. If it wasn't for that fact, I would literally kill them both. How do you guys wish to proceed?"

In this case, the F.B.I.'s efficiency was brisk and expeditious. In six months, they had the information needed to prosecute, and they did. Both aides were tried and convicted of spying and given the death penalty. Because of his diplomatic immunity status, Boris Gorbachov was under no indictment but was forced to leave the country for his role in the affair. As he as boarding his Learjet, he turned around for one last look at America, smiling at the barrage of cameras filming his departure and caught the eyes of a man standing in the back of the reporters staring at him intently and he now knew the face that went with the name his people were looking for. Willis Dash, and for the first time in as long as he could remember, he felt fear. He locked eyes with Willis and the fear engulfed him, mind, body and soul; it was a tangible thing. Willis's eyes radiated naked aggression as they bored into Gorbachovs' and then Willis mouthed the words in Russian, "I'm going to get you, watch."

****

Two years later, when Willis turned 16, Special Agent Katheryn Moore, true to her word, along with his father's signature, walked into the foyer of the Central Intelligence Agency with Willis at her side. When they entered, they entered to a thunderous roaring ovation. The entire area was filled with agents waiting for Willis' arrival. At the front of them all stood the director, J.T. Foss, with his hand extended for a handshake, and when Willis took it, he said, "Welcome home, son," and hugged him like he was, in fact, his father. After shaking at least, a hundred hands, Willis and Katheryn Moore were ushered into the director's office, where they sat. He gave Willis a general overview of the goings around the place and what he'd be doing until he was of age for fieldwork. Willis asked, "Do I get to choose my own spy's name?"

The director and Katheryn laughed, and he said, "Willis, we're not spying here; we are intelligence officers."

"So, you're telling me I can't be a spook? I want my code name to be The Spookster."

* * * * * * * * *

    Willis's two years of training went by quickly. He was amazed by the place, but they were more amazed by him and his abilities. They had never had an agent as smart as Willis, and not long after coming there, they started calling him the prodigal son. Two weeks after his 18th birthday, director Foss summoned him to his office. "Willis, when you first came here, you were 5' 6", 150 lbs. even. Now you are 6' 3," 225lbs, of pure strength, muscle, and intellect. You were given free rein to do as you please, and just like a kid in a candy store, you ate up everything in sight. A feat that I am extremely proud of. Never has an agent accomplished what you have in the amount of time you've had, and now is your time. I spoke to your father and told him of my plans for you, and you know what he said? He said to unleash the beast!" and pushed a folder across his desk to Willis, who picked it up and started perusing its contents greedily, it was literally his first time seeing anything top secret, and he was both amazed and humbled at the trust and belief in him that was being bestowed on him by the company. Foss continued: "Each name has what needs to be done next to it. Many of those names have been there for a long time because we haven't had the proper personnel to execute the operation. But with your language capabilities, we now do. I would like you to focus on the European names first, then work your way east. Choose anyone to work on and have at it. Your only requirement is that you work with the logistics office, so we know where you're going at all times and when to extract you if need be."

* * * * * * * * *

Boris Gorbachov entered his dacha in good spirits. He had just come back from the store where he'd bought caviar and wine, which his girlfriend Svetlana was so fond of. He entered his kitchen and saw the big man looking in his cupboard with his back toward him. Boris immediately opened his side kitchen cupboard and pulled out his gun, which he had hidden there, jacked a round in the chamber, pointed the gun at the man's back, and asked, "Who are you, and what do you want?" The man turned around slowly. His coat was open and hung loosely; in his waist, a gun butt protruded. His face looked slightly familiar.

"Is this the way you treat a guest?" asked the man in flawless Russian and nonchalantly pulled out a chair and sat down facing Boris.

"Who are you, and what is it you want?" asked Boris.

"Surely you remember me, comrade, don't you?" asked Willis. Slowly recognition dawned on Boris's face, and he went white with fear, then calmed down and smiled, remembering that he held the gun on the man.

"It was stupid of you to come here," said Boris.

"It is stupid of you to think you have the drop on me," said Willis.

"I don't see how, as you are alone, and I have the gun," said Boris.

"I have a gun also, Boris," said Willis.

"Yes, but mine is pointed at you," said Boris.

"Yes, it is pointed at me, but it's unloaded," said Willis and he opened his hand, showing the clip. Willis slid the clip across the table to Boris.

"If I wanted to kill you, I could have done so when you entered, but I didn't," said Willis.

"Why didn't you?" asked Boris.

"In exchange for your life, I want information," said Willis.

"I will not spy on my own country," he said.

"I'm not asking you to," said Willis.

"I have nothing to give you," said Boris.

"Then reach for the clip; let's see who's the fastest, old west style Boris; surely you've heard of the old west in your K.B.G. for dummies pamphlet?" Boris thought he might have been running a bluff, he pulled the trigger, and the hammer clicked on an empty chamber. Willis got up slowly and walked over to him. When he drew near enough, Boris swung the gun but violently, Willis grabbed his wrist as it came in its downward arc and twisted it with all his might, and it snapped with an audible crack. Boris screamed in pain, grabbed his wrist, and started crying, but said nothing; he just looked at Willis with tears running down his face. Boris was a big man, about 6' 5" and approximately 260lbs. Willis grabbed him by the lapels of his coat, heaved him up in the air, swung him around, and slammed him on the kitchen table, which broke under his weight and sent him crashing to the floor. Before he had a chance to even take a breath, Willis grabbed his foot and twisted violently, breaking his ankle. He howled in pain like a wounded moose. Willis tied him up. "A lot of people have done a lot of crying because of what you have done, and yet you have the nerve to cry?" asked Willis and pulled out a thin cylindrical metal tube bent in an arc shape about 8" long, attached at the end was a scalpel. "If you don't talk, I'm going to make sure you never talk again. I'm going to insert this into your mouth and slice your vocal cords to shreds; then I'm going to burn your eyes out like I did your buddy, Alexia. You see this?" and showed him a cigar cutter, "I'm going to use it to cut off your toes and your fingers. I'm going to systematically break every bone in your body; then, when you're lying there in excruciating pain, blind with no voice box to cry with, I'm going to waterboard you. So, Boris, the moral of the story is you will talk, even if you have to signal your answers; the question is when. I suggest you do it sooner than later, as you have a lot to lose."

"Okay, I'll talk," he said, not wanting to go through the torture.
"Good, now get to it," said Willis and began questioning him.

When Willis finished questioning him and was satisfied with his answers, Willis did everything he said he was going to do to him except waterboarding; there was no need for it. Willis then sat him upright in the kitchen between two drawers at head level, keeping his head from flopping to either side and snipped his spinal cord at the base of his neck. He left a note on his lap for whoever found him first, explaining about his neck injury so he could be kept alive. "See, Boris, I told you I'd get you, and you're going to learn how foul your own government is who you work for when it comes to the care you receive for your current condition."

THE YOUNG ADULT

Secrecy is paramount in intelligence work if an entity is to be successful in its undertaking of information gathering, or so I was thinking when I was perusing the files of open cases that needed enhancement or closure. As I was choosing my next assignment, the thought of the beautiful Katheryn Moore came to mind, and I put down the files I was viewing and headed to the computer room. I quickly accessed her files, having the top-secret clearance to do so. As I studied her files, I checked into the N.S.A. computers to see what they were up to, if anything, with Katheryn Moore. After comparing algorithms, I soon realized that not only was Ms. Moore's communications being monitored, so was the entire Homeland Security. They were under cyber-attack and apparently unaware of the breach of their systems, and neither was the N.S.A. aware of the breach; it was buried so sweetly. I raised the alarm and had everyone in the computer room launch various countermeasures to stop the intrusion and to try and locate the source's whereabouts... I also notified the N.S.A. to get them in on the hunt. I notified them by land line hoping not to put the hackers on point because part of their algorithms were cell phone intercepts. I then notified Homeland Security in the same manner.

This intrusion of the Homeland Securities system just ruined my spur-of-the-moment idea, which was to call Katheryn Moore and ask her for a date. I knew she would say yes but was unsure of how far she would go with me because she was ten years older than me. But before I could pursue my dream girl, I had to make sure she was safe, which meant I had to shut down the current attack against her agency. After several hours of relentless key tapping by all three agencies, the hacking ceased, and a trace revealed the source... I quickly assembled an impromptu team and went to dismantle the source's operation.

Chelyabinsk, Russia, three weeks later:

"Who are they, and what are they up to?" asked Victor, the boss, sharply.
"I do not know, comrade; they arrived a week ago, took over the warehouse approximately 2 miles southwest of town- the old mill plant- and since then, trucks have been coming and going, apparently making deliveries, as you can see from the photos. None of the men look familiar or are recognized through facial recognition

software, so they are definitely not Russian military," said Grecgov.

"I want 24-hour surveillance on them until we figure out who they are and what their business is here. Have a penetration team ready for a silent entry look around whenever they leave the premises unattended. I want pictures of what's inside. Make the entry clean- nothing taken- no trace of penetration, is that clear?" said Victor.

""Yes sir," replied his minions in unison.

After his subordinates left to undertake their mission, Commander Victor Vlademezko of the Russian underground movement sat at his desk with his feet on it, looking closely at the photos. His second in command, Lt. Cmdr. Ostap Kolov sat nervously a few feet away. He was nervous because he understood his commanders' violent moods and didn't want to get the brunt of his wrath. His commander was a brutal leader who expected results and anything short of success because of one's failings led to death. To commander Victor Vladvemezko death was the ultimate motivator. It suited his needs admirably, and everyone under his command knew it, which is why his orders were carried out to the enth. His success was legendary amongst his peers, which was why he held the position he did.

But the funny thing about Victor Vladvemezko was his stature. He was 5' 6", 210lbs., and looked like a little white rhino. His skin was extremely pale and pasty looking. He was completely bald and had no facial hair naturally, and cruel beady black eyes. He was wide and looked like a cinder block in the body. A thin mean looking slit was the only indication of a mouth.

"So, Ostap, do you think the K.G.B., or the G.R.U., are onto us here?" asked Victor.

"The faces match none that we have access to, that doesn't mean anything, they could be fresh out of the academy, or sleepers, only just awakened to infiltrate our operation. When our team penetrates their warehouse, we'll have all the info we need to determine who they are," said Ostap.

"If it's a secret branch of our government, what do you think we should do?" asked Victor to see how his second-in-command thought.

"Feed them disinformation. Killing them will only strengthen the government's resolve and make us even more outlawed and that's not what we want," said Ostap.

"You're half right, Ostap." said Victor.

"What's the other half?" asked Ostap.

"You'll see if they are the government. But in the meantime, think about it and let me know what you come up with," said Victor.

****

"Bennett, what do you think?" asked Mason, as we sat contemplating the ruse, which I dubbed "Operation Front."
"I think they are biting," replied Bennett.
"What do you think, Willis?" asked Mason.
"If they don't, we have wasted a lot of resources and money," replied Willis.
"Do you have a plan B?" asked Mason.
"Of course,' said Willis.
"Which is?" asked Bennett.
"We go raw dog, as they say in the hood," answered Willis.
"Willis, you can't be serious, that's a garrison sitting over there, and there are only three of us," said Mason.
"Which means we'll have our work cut out for us, won't we?" said Willis, smiling.
"Let's hope it doesn't come to plan B," said Bennett.
"Personally, I hope it does; it's been kind of boring lately," said Willis.

Operation Front was just that a front. We are playing German arms dealers with the hopes of infiltrating their ranks. Once in, sabotage was the order of the day for their main computer servers and maybe a death or two for good measure or maybe something different altogether.

"It's time to get the show on the road, gentlemen, let's go," said Willis.

"Where to?" asked Bennett.

"A quaint little pub on the other side of town," said Willis.

"You think they'll be there?" asked Mason.

"Of course, they'll follow us and, at the same time, send someone to break in and see what we're doing here," said Willis.

"What makes you think so?" asked Mason.

"It's what I'd do," said Willis. "Arm up and let's go; make sure the hidden cameras are working in real-time."

The penetration team was stunned. They entered through a second-story window and had to lower themselves down on a rope ladder, and as soon as they did, they were being recorded in real-time. They couldn't believe their eyes at what they were seeing. This could be a very serious situation for their movement, what they were seeing were weapons. Weapons which they knew their command would want. As they opened and closed crate after crate they were mesmerized. They took pictures and counted everything before they left, and they did it with precision and left thinking that their intrusion would go undetected.

As soon as we left, we were followed all the way to the pub, and soon after that, very conveniently, three hookers showed up-the game was afoot. I knew instinctively they were sent to engage us; we were posing as Germans. After about a half hour of fraternizing with the hookers, I went to the bathroom. Once inside, I cut my phone on and accessed the warehouse cameras; sure enough, we had visitors- two of them prowled around taking pictures. Fine. The fish had taken the bait. Just as I was about to exit the bathroom, I heard the door at the back open, held fast, and heard the slow, plodding footsteps of a man going by and out to the bar area. When I came out of the bathroom, I saw the wet footprints heading into the bar. By the length of his stride, I saw that he was a big man, at least as big as me. As I neared the doorway, I stood at an angle and peered out. I spotted him immediately because of his size, and he was surreptitiously watching the hallway to the bathroom where he was. This told me he was told I was here.

He was a big fella like I thought, at least 6' 6" and close to 300lbs. I walked up to the bar where he sat and ordered another drink, making sure my Russian was broken and acted like I was drunk. I then sat on a stool

at the bar leaning back on it facing the small dance floor and said to myself loud enough for him to hear, "Russian women are so beautiful, even the whores," and kept looking at the women in the place. The big fella said, "Yes, they are, your Russians not so goods where are you from, if I may ask?"
"Berlin," I replied.
"If you don't mind me asking, what's your name?" asked the big man.
"Kurt, and yours?" I replied.
"Ivan," he said. "What brings you here?" he asked.
"Business, the climate here is good for it, so you live near here?" I asked.
"Yes, all my life. What kind of business are you into?" he asked.
"Toys," I said, "And you?" I asked half drunkenly.
"The revolution," he said.
"Really? That's very interesting stuff. Dangerous too," I said.
"I must go now. Thank you for the time; enjoy your evening. Maybe we'll meet again some time," and he got up and left. I rejoined my team, and we stood awhile longer, then left ourselves.
"Commander Vladvemezko," said Grecgov, "The infiltration teams report is as follows: Inside the warehouse are German arms. Everything from rocket launchers to

handguns and ammo for all. The official count of all the armaments is as follows, 40 cases of rocket launchers and 60 cases of rockets for such. Each crate has 6 rocket launchers, and each rocket case had ten rockets, 60 cases of machine guns, 60 cases of handguns and 40 cases of mortars, approximately a thousand grenades, and as many land mines, sir."

"Thank you, Grecgov," said Vladvemezko. "Send in Ivan."

"Yes sir," said Gregcov and left. A few minutes later, Ivan entered, after knocking, and without preamble, began: "Sir, the subjects are German Nationalists I believe."

"Why?" asked Vladvemezko.

"I instinctively felt the militariness about them; the one I spoke to, who I believe is the boss, told me they were selling toys and isn't that exactly what they have in the warehouse, sir?" asked Ivan.

"Thank you, Ivan, you're dismissed," said Vladvemezko without answering his question. After he left Vladvemezko paced his office in deep contemplation with Ostap sitting to the side, saying nothing.

"Ostap, what do you think?" asked Vladvemezko.

"They might be the German secret police- the Stasi," said Ostap.

"If that were the case, I'm quite sure they'd be sympathetic to our cause- they don't like the current Russian government, and if they were to help us that would build good relations with us once we take control of our government," said Vladvemezko.

"But suppose they are not Stasi?" asked Ostap.

"That's the problem, Ostap, exactly who are they? German Nationalists just trying to make money or Stasi trying to infiltrate our ranks?" said Vlavemezko.

"We could always over run the warehouse and take everything and kill them," said Ostap.

"Yes, that thought came to mind. But if they are legitimate businessmen, we have a golden opportunity to procure weapons. Surely, they have anti-tank weaponry and maybe even anti-aircraft weaponry too. We need to watch them further to establish their credibility and take it from there. Continue surveillance, Ostap, you're dismissed," said Vladvemezko.

"Yes, sir," said Ostap, leaving to carry out his orders.

One week later:

Two trucks pulled to the warehouse and took turns backing in to be loaded; then the two trucks took off on their journey. As expected, the Russians followed. The trucks made their way to the foot of the Ural Mountains and stood there for several hours before the plane arrived. It was a German airbus freight plane. The contents of the trucks were loaded on board and the plane then took off and headed south. This was recorded by the Russians who themselves were being recorded. The trucks then went back to the warehouse.

"Sir, the plane in question was tracked by a hacked satellite to Libya," said Ostap.
"They appear to be legitimate businessmen," said Vladvemezko.
"Yes sir, they must have connections. If we were to connect with them, surely, they could somehow connect with the Stasi," said Ostap.
"Send in Ivan to make their acquaintance. Tell him to be blunt; time is of the essence. We need to have access to a broader spectrum of weaponry. Tell him if he can, to get him to come here to make a deal," said Victor Vladvemezko.
"Yes, sir," said Ostap and left.
"Do you think they took the bait?" Mason asked.

"Yes, now we'll wait for them to devise a way to make contact without scaring us off." I said, "Call in the rest of the team."

One week later:

We traveled in a three-car convoy to the best restaurant in the city. When we got there, Mason and Bennett got out and stood out front while the driver went inside to recon the place. The men in the two other cars got out and placed themselves strategically up and down the sidewalk, obviously for security. The driver returned from the restaurant and gave the all-clear signal, and we entered. Our outer security blanket advised me by phone that we were being followed, which I knew would be the case. "Good," I said to myself, "they will attempt to make contact tonight. Predictable."

About a half hour later, who walks in but Ivan. He had a nice pretty ash blonde on his arm, and when he saw me, he feigned surprise and sauntered over. After we exchanged pleasantries, I asked him to join us, and he did. The girl's name was Svetlana, and she was a real looker, this one. She was the talk of the place in minutes, and Ivan took advantage of this and used it as his in to start the conversation.

"You like Comrade Kurt?"

"Yes, she's beautiful," I said.

"You can have her for a small price," said Ivan.

"While she's beautiful, I'm here on business," I said.

"Yes, it is what makes the world go around these days, and I'd like to purchase some of your toys," he said. I looked at him hard, acting like I was unsure of his intent and said.

"What are you looking for in particular? Do you have a son or daughter?" I responded.

He laughed lightly and said, "It is good that you don't trust me, as you don't know who I am, and I don't know who you truly are either, but I do know of the toys you sell. I've been sent here as an emissary to broker a deal with you. If you wish to deal strictly with the boss, that is fine too. The choice is yours."

"Who are you and who's your boss, and what kind of deal are we talking about?" I said.

"I am who I say I am, Ivan; my boss's name is Victor Vladvemezko of the Russian Liberation Army, and the deal we wish to make is for weapons, what you refer to as toys," he said. I sat as if stunned in silence, looking at him, and he looked back at me without blinking. Finally, I said, "How do I know you're not the police, K.G.B or G.R.U., How do I know you're really Russian liberation Army?"

"If I were any of those, your warehouse on Stuzdurn street would already have been raided, and you and your friends here would be sitting in a precinct having an altogether different conversation. I think you know I'm not K.G.B. or G.R.U. because you must have contact with the Stasi and probably had me checked out when we first met, a man in your business can never be too careful," he said.

"Of course, you are right; before I make any deals with you, I will definitely need to verify who you are and your boss too. I will check with my contacts to do so, and take it from there," I said, and we exchanged phone numbers. After that, the night went well.

****

"Well Kurt, what do you think of my compound?" asked Vladvemezko, after showing me around and out lining what he needed, which was anti-tank and anti-aircraft weaponry.

"You certainly picked a defendable position, and your spot on to your weakness which is from the air and rounds fired from tanks. I think you should have another such base-a fallback position- don't put all your eggs in one basket, as they say," I said.

"I do; that place is top secret," he said with a smile, and I smiled back and said, "Yes, I can help you with what you need, and will for the right price," as we came by a room filled with computers being operated. That is just what I was looking for, my objective. "Do you know I can get you a supercomputer too?" I asked.

"Really?" he asked interestedly.

"Yes, it's called the **CRAY 2**, and once programmed can do the work of every person in that room in less than ten minutes. Really a fine piece of machinery." He changed directions and walked into the room full of computers, and I looked at my watch and pressed the magic button slyly, which locked in the exact coordinates into my G.P.S. tracking system. Mission accomplished. We then sat down to discuss business in his office over a nice meal. After eating and desultory conversation Valdvemezko got up and opened a wall safe and took out a velvet sack, closed the safe, sat back down and pushed the sack over to me and told me to open it and took a small soup bowl and gave it to me too, and told me to pour the contents into it. I did and was stunned at what came out-diamonds, about 50 of them, in all different colors. They glittered marvelously, reflecting the light. I was no expert on the jewelry, but by their size, there had to be at least twenty-five million dollars' worth, far more than the agreed-upon price of 11 million.

"We are literally short on cash. So, I would ask you two things; the first is that since you would have to resell these stones to make your money, you take two million extra for the inconvenience, and second, that you sell the rest and give me the cash and take another million as your commission. Each of those diamonds varies in size from 40 to 50 carrots, there's sixty-four of them," he said.

"You would trust me with these?" I asked.

"I did my research on you. Your reputation is excellent. Besides, there is nowhere on this earth that I cannot find you. Besides, there is plenty more where those came from, and it's a win-win for us both, something I'm quite sure you're into," he said. "Deal!" I said with a smile, and we shook on it. After a pleasant evening, I rebagged the stones and left to execute the rest of my plan.

* * * * * * * * *

Quietly and unobserved, Bennett, Mason and I, and a couple of others slipped out of the warehouse and drove 50 miles due south and came to our other warehouse. Inside was a gulf stream jet and a big truck. I told them to warm the jet up, put it on the runway, and wait. Bennett and I took the truck about 100 yards away from the jet. Mason and Bennett removed the tarp, and I went to the control panel and went to work. I warmed up the control system completely, then raised the programmed G.P.S. coordinates in accordance with my watch and watched as the hydraulics lifted the massive scud missile to an angle of about 47 degrees stopped, programmed it to fire in 8 minutes, then we ran to the jet and boarded. I took control of the jet, and we picked up speed for takeoff, and as soon as we did, we all saw the flash of ignition of the scud as it took off. I left banked gaining altitude as I did so to pursue the scud to see if we got a direct hit because scuds were notoriously inaccurate past a hundred miles, but our target was 50 miles, and we hoped the scud would go true.

The scud was faster than the gulf stream and took only 5 minutes to reach the target. We saw the brilliant flash of light of the explosion ahead and the plume of fire and smoke as we neared, and because it was night if anyone was still alive would hear our jet as it buzzed the sight, but not being able to see due to darkness, would automatically think the strike came from a Russian military craft, or so I hoped. When we buzzed the sight, we could see the entire back side of the building where the computers were ruined and ablaze. Amazingly the front portion where Vladvemezkos office was undamaged. I turned eastward towards my next mission.

When the scud hit the compound Commander Victor Vladvemezko, Ostap and Ivan were discussing their next course of action against the government once the weapons were delivered. The sound of the blast and the concussion threw them all out of their seats, and they hit the floor simultaneously but alive. They all stood still, and they heard the jet fly by, The Russians are coming," said Ostap, who got up and ran to the door, opened it looking back over his shoulder at the others, then turned forward and tried to stop, but it was too late, his momentum took him forward and he fell straight down because the hallway was gone. It was only a one-flight drop, but he had the unfortunate luck to land on a jagged piece of wood about 6' long and impaled himself, dying instantly. Vladvemezko and Ivan, after seeing Ostaps fate, went to the back window, climbed down and fled.   His remaining troops fled also. After two days without the Russians showing up, they came back with trucks to salvage anything they could. When that was done, they went to the warehouse. After a few minutes, it was apparent that no one was in the warehouse. Ivan, who was in charge, ordered it looted. They cleaned it out, it took three trips to do so, but they did it. Three weeks later, in preparation to attack a Russian base in retaliation for their attack on the compound, they were checking the weapons and realized that none of them worked; they were, literally, toys, look alike toys. Commander Victor Vladvemezko was livid. Furiously angry at finding out the weapons were fake. He called his contact number Kurt only to find out that it was dial a joke. He'd been duped by the Russian military, probably the **K.G.B.**, out of 50 million in diamonds and half his complex destroyed. He sent out the word throughout the entire underground of Russia and Germany to find Kurt Merkel. Ten million dollars was the prize, and then waited. He felt in his heart that it was only a matter of time before he found Kurt Merkel. He would torture him and his entire family for duping him so. He would pay.

THE ADULT

I was perusing the file before me and didn't like what I saw. It was obvious what was going on. Someone was killing C.I.A. agents stationed in Europe, in general. Six so far, which meant a leak. Director Foss sat in front of me at his desk, obviously brooding over the situation.

"The reason this file didn't come to you sooner, Willis, is because it was already an active party investigation, with Sullivan on the lead, but as you can see, he's dead now too."
"I'll take it," I said.
"What's your plan of action, Willis?" said Director Foss. "I'll mimic Sullivans every step- go abroad to a station and await the killer to come for me, and when he does, I'll make him talk, then kill him, his boss, and his boss's secretary for good measure," I said.
"This is a top priority mission, Willis, seriously urgent. Figure it out and clear it up pronto. Keep Logistics up to date. Mason and Bennett will ride shotgun for you. Always coordinate your movements with them. I do not want to explain my condolences to your father. I'm quite sure he does not want to hear them, and I don't want to say them." Said Director Foss.

* * * * * * * * *

I studied the files of all the men that were killed, trying to pinpoint a connection but could see nothing definitive, state side. So, I followed in their footsteps, checking in with all the agents that they did. I even went to linguistics to brush up on my Russian, even though I didn't have too, because it was flawless, and besides, the instructor was an older chick that flirted with me every time I saw her in passing. I also checked in with the state department as this was a sanctioned operation.

To me, Moscow was an ugly place. Its over crowdedness and characterless middle eastern architecture reflect the real mind set of the Russian. The Kremlin reminded me of the Taj Mahal, and I couldn't help but wonder if it was a sign of what was coming for the Russian people. I went on about the business of being a Dutch businessman making my contacts and forwarding sensitive information back to the states. I followed protocol to the letter waiting for what was to come. Mason and Bennett were never far off, and I thought maybe they were made, and that was what was stopping an attempt on my life. The agents that were killed were killed in a variety of different ways to cover up what was going on. I didn't think the K.G.B. would kill so many operatives; they knew that would draw attention-too much attention. This must be a lone wolf operation Of a G.R.U. Provocation. I was sitting in Gorky Park feeding the pigeons on an unseasonably mild day when I realized I was under surveillance.

She came sauntering up, walking a French poodle, sat down a few feet away, and lit a cigarette. She was beautiful too, and I recognized her. Her name was Natasha Nicovich; she was a G.R.U. Trained agent working for Colonel Arcadia Yemkova. A very dangerous man, by all accounts. Instinctively I knew l had hit pay dirt. I kept doing what I was doing and just waited for the play that I knew would come, and it did.
"Such a nice day, don't you think?" she asked, looking over at me as if she were really interested in me. I looked at her, pulled out my Russian translation book, and replied in a bungled manner like a tourist.
"Could you please say again? I did not understand you," she gave me a beautiful smile and repeated what she said, and so started the game of cat and mouse. She told me her name was Myzza, and I told her I was

Michael. We parlayed for a while then I begged off, promising to call her soon so she could show me around a bit before I went back to Holland. I spoke to Bennett through my watch as I walked away, instructing him to follow her and for Mason to stay with me and watch my six.

Two weeks later, I was in a quaint little cafe when my phone buzzed, it was Bennett. "Natasha and two agents are one block away, around the corner. She's getting out of the car apparently heading your way. She has something in the palm of her right hand. Be careful," and hung up.

I came out of the cafe and headed her way. It was a dark, dank evening and not many people were about. She came walking up, feigning surprise at seeing me, "Michael," she said, "What a surprise-why haven't you called me?" with her arms outstretched for me to take them. But instead of taking her hands in mine, I reached forward with both my arms outstretched and grasped the back of her hands and pulled her forward as though I was going to hug her, but instead, as she came forward and went to put her right hand on my waist, I held it fast and twisted it. I broke her wrist. She gasped in pain and tried to knee me in the nuts. I parried the blow by twisting my thigh in front of it and hit her with a vicious elbow. I heard the bone crack as her jaw broke. I grabbed the back of her head, pulling her downward and came up with a knee at the same time, which took her in the throat, smashing her windpipe. She choked to death right there. I called Bennett and ordered him to silent six the two men now, hung up, and dragged Natasha to the corner. When I looked down the block, I saw Bennett shooting a silenced two rounds into the car. I put Natasha in the back seat and ordered Bennett and Mason to the embassy and out of Russia on the next plane. I would stay and complete the mission.

* * * * * * * * *

The next morning, I entered the G.R.U. headquarters in the full regalia of a K.G.B. General, something not regularly seen at G.R.U. headquarters. I walked in with purpose, and a young officer at the desk stood up, saluted, and asked who I was here to see. I stopped, glared at him menacingly, and asked, "Would you like to be stationed at Ice station Zebra in Siberia?" In flawless Russian.
"No, sir!" he replied, obviously shaken up.
"I didn't think so," I said and walked on.

Colonel Arcadia Yemkov was nervous, and he didn't know why. He was sitting in his office sipping on his morning coffee, contemplating the information about the killings of his three agents last night, when the General walked in, he was just about to issue an arrest warrant for the American C.I.A. agent posing as a Dutch businessman named Michael Schmidt.

"I am General Demetri Volkov, K.G.B. get me the files on the three agents of yours that were killed Last night," he said without preamble and sat down. While Yemkov had never seen Volkov before, he'd heard of him, and from that knew him to be a very influential man, at the politburo, had the director's ear. If that wasn't enough, he would put him in Lubyanka if he even acted like he didn't like his presence, so he got up immediately without hesitation and opened his safe to get the files. He opened the safe and was about to close it when I told him not to.

"Just sit. I have a few questions," I said.

"Yes, Sir," replied Yemkov. I sat faking like I was really reading the files and said, "Tell me about the operation-in detail," and he did, including how he got the information about the operatives. As he spoke, I got up and paced around his office with my hands behind my back, Russian style. I could sense his nervousness. He was scared as he knew his operation was unsanctioned. When he finished outlining the entire operation, and my pacing brought me directly behind him, I grabbed him in one quick movement from behind and snapped his neck, killing him instantly. He had a standard issue rucksack in the corner. I took it, put the files in it, emptied the safe of all the files, and then locked it back. I looked in the other draws and file cabinets for anything intellectually feasible and took a couple of other labeled files. I then exited his office. His secretary got up and saluted smartly. I told him to carry my bag for me, and as soon as he gave me his back, I broke his neck too and killed him just like I said I would. I exited the building unhindered and made haste to get out of the country. I decided to stay away from the embassy because as soon as the bodies were discovered, the security apparatus was sure to have them covered like a blanket. I made my way to Germany, then to London, where I took a company plane straight to Langley to have the information disseminated.

* * * * * * * *

I had all the agents pertinent to the dead agent's investigation gathered in our situation room to discuss the progress I had made in the case.

"Dearly beloved," I began, "We are gathered here today in the mutual interest of finding out who has been selling our agents out to their deaths. Good men they were, one and all. Today with your help I hope to weed out the mole and put an end to the breach that has cost us so dearly."

"From the outset I had the feeling that the Russians were not getting on to us because of good work on their behalf and that was proven to me on my foray into their clutches, and they didn't have a clue that I was there. The K.G.B. whose job it is didn't have a clue that I was in the country but somehow or another, the G.R.U. did and didn't share this information with the K.G.B., but instead attempted to kill me as they did our compatriots in unsanctioned hits. Very unprofessional because they didn't even attempt to squeeze any information from our people, just kill them. This is what made me realize that we had a mole here, home, the one place where we are supposed to be safe. While on my foray I did get a lead on the source of the problem. It came to me that the mole was a sleeper cell that had been awakened, and furthermore I had a name. But the name was a Russian name, long since changed since they were planted here in the states. But even though it was changed, sympathy for the motherland of Russian never dwindled and grew deeply in one of the children, until one day, that child, who had become an adult, had gotten a job here, and had access to the names of the agents going abroad.

"But I still had one problem, I didn't know the double agent's American name. I did though procure a picture of that agent as a child with the uncle, who is the late Colonel Arcadia Yemkov of **G.R.U.**, who was running the operation that killed our men." As I was speaking, I moved around the room slowly until I was slightly behind everyone in the room. Then tension started to mount as the agents sensed the culprit was about to be revealed.

"I draw your attention to the big screen at the front of the room for your help in identifying the mole." And hit my phone and the big screen came to life with a 4' x 6' photo on the left side and an empty 4' x 6' box on the right next to it. Everyone's attention was rapt to it except one person who took one look at it then put her head down. No one noticed except me because I was looking at her and everyone else was looking at the picture. It was a family picture with the colonel and his wife, their three children, and the colonel's brother and his wife and their four children. Everyone just looked trying to figure out who the mole was. Finally, I said, "I know the suspense is killing you, so I'll not hold off any longer. The first thing I ask is no shooting because the culprit is unarmed. In the empty box will appear a computer-generated age progression image of our mole." I hit the button and when it came on everyone looked at it and in unison turned around and looked at the linguistics agent, Dawn Griffin. I'll give it to her though, she was in a bad predicament, but held her head high with a tear rolling down one side of her face. Two female agents got up and went over to her and yanked her out of her chair. One slapped her so hard it smeared her lipstick. The other one punched her in the stomach. I stopped the onslaught. "Take her to debriefing room four and have the water board ready," I said. Just then an undersecretary stuck her head through the door. Agent Dash, I have a secure line call for you from Agent Katheryn Moore, Homeland Security."

"Be right there," I said and wondered lustily about the beautiful Katheryn Moore whom I hadn't seen in four years.

THE WAXSTER

It's been four years since I'd seen Katheryn Moore, the beautiful Katheryn Moore. I asked her for a date, and she said yes. I was like a kid in a candy store dreaming of what was to come when the phone rang. It was director Foss-he wanted to see me immediately and instinctively I knew my date with the beautiful Katheryn Moore would have to be shelved and I wasn't the least bit happy about it. In fact, I was pissed.
"I received a call from the president, Willis, and he directed me to put my best man on the 'Waxster' case," said director Foss, pushing a file folder over to me as I sat down.
"In the movies, when the boss pushes a file over, it's supposed to say, 'top-secret' on it- how come this one doesn't?" I asked, smiling.
"Because, for one, this is not the movies and two, it's really not top-secret Willis," said Foss," smiling back.
"Well, then I can't help you- I only do 'top-secret' stuff- I'm a spook remember? But why is the president directing us? Doesn't he have confidence in the F.B.I.?" I asked.
"Three of the victims are family members of congressmen," said Foss.

"Oh, I get it; it's getting too close to home," I said.
"The Spookster to the rescue," said Foss.

I called Katheryn and gave her the bad news, and she was not happy about it either. I promised her though, that as soon as I cleared this thing up, I'd be there sitting on her doorstep, waiting for her to come home. If anything, else came up I'd quit before I let it get in the way of me seeing her again.

* * * * * * * * *

A serial killer was on the loose; the media had dubbed him the "Waxster" because he encased all his victims in wax with candles sticking out of their orifices and left them in open-topped cages, on display, for all to see when discovered. So far, 26 victims have been attributed to him. His boundaries knew no limits. His victims were from 26 states so far and found in states other than their own.

So now, for the first time, I will delve into domestic violence, and I relished the opportunity to match wits with this psychopath they're calling the "Waxster" who likes making waxed mannequins out of everyday ordinary working people for who knows what reason. Motivation is usually key in solving such matters, but I didn't care one whit about the dude's motivation. I was going to find him by good old guesswork. For this case, the F.B.I. had selected its New York field office as its base of operations, so I went there to review the evidence they had amassed thus far, and once that was done, I'd let my mind do the walking.

* * * * * * * * *

A briefing was in progress about the current status of the Waxster case when I arrived.
"Who are you, and why are you late?" said the agent at the head of the room.
"Special agent Jack Lord-Hawaii five O - I'm late because my osprey had only one engine working, my pilot and I flew at a forty-five-degree angle the entire trip. I feel like I'm sitting sideways right now- hey your arsenal have any levelers? I need to level off," I said. Quite a few people were giggling, and someone yelled out, "Try lisa in accounting- she'll level you right off."
"Roger that," I yelled back.
"Okay, Special agent Jack Lord from Hawaii five 0 - what's your expertise?" said the speaker up front.
"Psychism 101, I practice it and preach it myself all the time," I said. Just then, the

door opened, and a man walked briskly to the front; there was something vaguely familiar about his walk, and I realized what it was when he turned around. It was none other than Special Agent Conner Rawlings. I told myself to be calm because I didn't like him, nor did he like me.

"Gentlemen," he said without preamble, "We have our 27th victim" and went on to outline the situation as best he knew it from the preliminary reports he'd been given. When he finished, he looked around the room, making eye contact with everyone, and when he spotted me, I saw the flicker of irritation cross his eyes momentarily, and he said, "You is it?"

"Me?" I said, feigning astonishment, "I'm Special Agent Jack Lord, N.C.I.S. Hawaii, Psych Division, genius at your service."

Conner Rawlings opened his phone and started making calls. Everyone was wondering what was going on because something was definitely going on between the two of us. After talking on his phone for about twenty minutes, he turned around, seething mad and said, "Good to have you aboard, Special Agent Jack Lord," and directed an underling to take me to the computer room where I was given a desk with a P.C. and a whole stack of hard copy files of all the victims, along with a whole bunch of other stuff.

I sat at the desk and looked around at the hustle and bustle of activity going on around me. Police detection is at its best when all the different agencies are working for one common cause; apparently, it wasn't working. The Waxster had claimed another victim.

The edge I had over everyone here was my powers of observation. Because of how my mind worked, I could see patterns where there apparently none were. My first order of business was to figure out how he chose his victims; once I figured that out, I would look for a thread that connected them all-the proverbial needle in the haystack. But it might not be that hard to detect the needle; at least, I didn't think so. The victims ranged in age from 19 to 40. None of the victims knew each other. There were 18 women and nine men. The only thing that connected the women was that they all had thigh gaps-something a deviant mind would most certainly be attracted to. So, sex was a factor in this creep's mind set. The men themselves were all openly homosexual. That in itself is motivation, as homosexuals have been persecuted since the beginning of time.

I thought long and hard about these two facts, and a picture formed in my mind, albeit fuzzy. To a demented mind, a woman's thigh gap could probably be a trigger. Maybe he was the product of an abusive mother who had a thigh gap, and to get back at her; he would kill women with thigh gaps. Maybe he was molested as a boy by a man dressed in drag, so he killed women and men as victims. None of the victims were sexually abused carnally, though, so why are the candles sticking out the orifices? All the victims had small candles sticking out of their ears and noses and 10" candles sticking out their mouths and anus and vaginas. The significance of this I had yet to grasp, but I would. A small tag with a string, the same size as the ones on t-bags, read, in typed lettering, "The clouds always dim the candles." I wondered idly at those words trying to grasp their true meaning. All serial killers have a signature, and the signature tells you why he's doing what he's doing and who he is. You just have to figure out the significance of the signature, which, more often than not, is never figured out by investigators. Most of the time, having caught the perpetrator by other means, the perpetrator then tells his story and the significance of the signature. I hoped that wasn't the case cause if it was, it might be a long time before we caught this phsyco.

The victims had been placed in regular iron-barred cages with open tops. The cages gleamed as if they'd just been professionally polished. They were of all different kinds and heights and diameters; I guess to fit the victims. All the industries where such cages were made were under investigation, and instinctively, I knew that would draw a blank. So, I wasn't going to look into it because this guy was apparently too smart to leave such an obviously mundane trail as that.

Next, I thought about the logistics and the risks of abducting a person in one state, taking him wherever to mummify them, and then taking that person or body to another state to put on display. Very risky. He could be using any manner of trucking; that is a mission in itself. It would be very hard to isolate one truck out of the thousands that travel on the highways and byways of America daily. But I had a good idea how I could attempt to do that. There was nothing to distinguish the victim's money wise-they ranged from the rich to the poor—and apparently, no one was immune from his transgressions. I poured over all the files for twelve hours straight, over back-to-back cups of coffee. When I finally finished, I had a definitive plan of action. I'd first go to Fairfax, West Virginia, to look at the

Waxster's creation, where the bodies were being kept. I wanted to look at The Waxster's creations to see if I could get a feel of how he moved or any idea that came to mind.

* * * * * * * * *

The latest victim of the Waxster, Carl Folkes, woke up drowsy and disoriented—he didn't know where he was. The constant banging from rough travel had woken him. He yelled at the top of his lungs for hours on end, but it was to no avail. After being in the dark box tied up for hours and no one answering his yells, he started to feel real fear. Fear of the unknown and uncertainty of the future can be a tangible thing; to Carl Folkes, he felt it now. He started crying. Carl had no idea how long he was in the box. He felt the traveling stop for a couple of minutes and could make out a low humming sound, then felt his box being pushed on wheels. A while later, it stopped and began to rise upright. The box then opened, and the brightness of the powerful overhead lights blinded him. When his vision cleared, he looked around. A man in all white stood with his back to Carl, going through a medicine cabinet. Carl looked around the room before speaking; it was a big room. At the far end, a welding machine stood opposite a galvanizer used in metal furniture shops. Piles of irons of all shapes and sizes were stacked neatly to one side. There were all kinds of stuff in that room. He looked down at himself; he was strapped in a coffin. He looked on as the man turned around, and he froze in even more fear. The man had on a wax mask—the mask of a jackal. He walked to Carl and stopped in front of him. "Hello, Carl Folkes, I am Anubis, and I am here to Shepard you to the underworld," said the man.

"Anubis? Please, mister, please, I'm begging you, let me go; I won't tell a soul, I swear," said Carl, stammering in fear.

"Of course, you're not telling anyone anything, you're not going anywhere, but where we all go, I'm here to escort you there— I am Anubis," said the man stoically.

"Please, mister Anubis, please!" Carl yelled shrilly.

"I am here to escort you to the underworld; I am Anubis," said the man. Carl broke down in tears, realizing he was in the hands of the Waxster.

"What did I do? I'm not a bad person, I," Anubis cut him off.

"You are an abomination in the creator's eyes- you must go to the underworld; I am Anubis, I will escort you there."

* * * * * * * * *

The bodies were set up in three rows evenly spaced, nine apiece. It was like a wax museum for real, except instead of pure wax figurines, these were actual people encased in wax. I walked up and looked at the first one. The tag said Sarah Darby. She was set in a triangular cage, 3x3x3x4. She stood with one hand on each corner, slightly bent over with her back arched inwards, pushing her butt up in the air. She stood, ankles touching and even though they were touching, I could see her thigh gap, and I knew instinctively that was by design. Sticking out her orifices and mouth were pink swirl candles 10" long and 1" wide. Out of her ears and nostrils, 4" long thin gray candles protruded.

I stood there staring at Sarah Darby, who was Senator Richard Lewis' niece, willing her to point me in the right direction, but nothing came to mind. Injections of different kinds of chemicals killed all the victims. Sarah Darby was lucky in that respect; she was injected with a pocket of air in her bloodstream that, once it went to her heart, killed her almost instantaneously—very little pain. I looked at the tea bag sized tag that hung from her right ear candle with the words: "The clouds always dim the candles," and wondered what it meant and would continue to wonder till I figured it out. I passed a few more, wondering idly about what I was seeing. One victim, Percy McIntyre, was in a round cylindrical open-top cage about 7' tall. He was a tall man, appx. 6' 3" 220 lbs. He was in the act of shooting a waxed basketball. It wouldn't have been so morbid if it wasn't for the candles. This nut sought to portray death as an art, using unwilling participants to mimic life in his version of death.

The detail in the sculptures was amazing I thought as I looked at Denise Metcalf. He captured her essence perfectly, I thought. Denise Metcalf in real life was a lady of the night, a prostitute, and even in death, she looked like one, thanks to the sure steady hands of the Waxster. She lay on a wax cot on her left side. Her head rested in the palm of her left hand, which was holding it up as she looked through sightless eyes. Her right leg was going straight up in the air, with her right arm holding it up behind the knee. She had a garter belt on and lace-up heels. Her left breast lay exposed, obviously slipping out the bra— the right one almost doing the same thing; the detail was amazing, and once again, the only flaw was the derogatory placement of the candles. Her cage was rectangular and 7' tall; obviously, she was supposed to be a caged animal. She was taken from Wichita, Kansas and found on the Northern most ledge of the Grand Canyon, obviously on prominent display.

The next one was a girl of 19. She was a world-class gymnast named Natasha Green. She was bent over backward with her right hand holding her up and her left straight up in the air; she was in a wide barred octagon cage. She was from Texas and was found in an inflatable raft lolling on current on the Arkansas River.
"What do you think is this guy's deal?" asked the escorting officer. I glanced at him and didn't see or feel any guile in him, so I responded in kind.
"He wants to immortalize his victims in death the way they lived in life," I said.
"I'm no expert, but he seems very talented with his hands. Why didn't he just sculpt the people? Why did he have to put the actual bodies in? What are the candles about?" He asked.
"He wanted to immortalize the person, literally. I think the candles, if lit, would merely continue the deceit by keeping the sculptures viewable. I also think the candles are symbolic of his impotence, which is why

he didn't light them. He didn't rape or sodomize any of the victims," I said.

"I didn't know wax was so hard," he said.

"It isn't. He placed steel rods at strategic points in the bodies to keep them in the positions he wanted." I answered.

"What do you think he means by the clouds always dims the candles?" he asked.

"That is another detail that eludes me—for now," I answered.

I looked at every sculptured victim committing the details to memory for future reference. I came to the latest one— it came in yesterday- Carl Folkes. Carl Folkes worked in Silicon Valley — a computer tech— and by all accounts, a whiz. His sculpted body was found at the base of Mesa Verde in Northern Arizona. Like all the male victims, Carl was homosexual, and I wondered how the Waxster chose his victims and got close to them to subdue them. I had to figure out how he was moving them across state lines.

* * * * * * * * *

When I was on my way back to the airport when I pulled up to a red light. In the back seat of the car on my left, two kids, a boy and a girl were arguing furiously over a laptop.

"Mommy, Tommy won't let me use it!" said the girl indignantly.

"Tattletale!" said the boy sticking his tongue out at his sister.

"Thomas, why can't you share with your sister?" said the mother, "Let her use it for a change; she's your sister." The boy got mad for a minute but passed it to her.

"It's not working, mommy!" said the girl looking at it.

"Yes, it is, it's cloudy; once the clouds move, you'll see the earth," said the boy. They were looking at google earth. The light changed, and they moved off, and I said to myself, "Thank you, Tommy," as I pulled off too and memorized their license plate number.

Instead of going back to New York, I went to Langley, back to the company, because thanks to Tommy, I now had a good plan of action. I went to see director Foss and explained what I wanted to be done. He green-lighted it immediately. I had 26 agents in the computer room: "As you all know, we've been asked to assist in the apprehension of the notorious Waxster, and we will succeed where everyone else has failed. I want each of you to view recorded google earth footage of the victim's name in front of you. I want you to see if you can't pick up and track the victim before his or her abduction. Failing that, I want you to list any suspicious vehicles in or around the victim's last known location. I also want you to review the area where they were found for the vehicle that brought them there. It will not be easy and will take a while, as apparently, bad weather was present at all the locations where the bodies were found. Good luck— let's get to it." I said.

I sat at my terminal and went to work myself pursuing another hunch. I was at it for about 20 minutes when a new young agent, Hilary Eubanks, came over to me.
"Agent Dash, may I speak to you for a minute?" she asked excitedly.
"Sure Ms. Eubanks—call me Willis," I said.
"Only if you call me Hilary," she said with a smile— she liked me.
"Okay, Hilary, what's on your mind?" I said.
"The weather was bad at all the victim's last known locations and where they were found. I checked all the victims, and it was the same with all of them. Extensive cloud coverage. I also realized that the Waxster always takes his victims to another state where there is cloud coverage, and I believe that he does that to use the cloud coverage so he cannot be tracked by satellites, which he knows law enforcement has access to and would use to track him if they could." she said.

"Don't we have satellites that can track through clouds?" I asked.

"Yes, but they work on thermal imaging— we wouldn't be able to see the make or model or a plate number of a vehicle when cloudy," she said.

"Thank you, Hilary; now we know that he travels with his victims only in inclement weather to avoid satellite detection, so he can put them on display without being observed," I said.

"One more thing, Willis, pertaining to the satellites," she said.

"Yes, Hilary?" I said.

"I think I figured out what the Waxster meant when he said, 'The Clouds always dim the candles' on the tag and why he said it," she said.

"In case you didn't notice, I'm all ears," I said, rapt and fascinated at the insight she was providing me with.

"The lens on the satellite shoots pinpoint beams of light at night to the surface of the planet, the beam is so thin it's not noticeable to the human eye on the ground as it passes by. Through a series of mirrors, the satellite magnifies the beam, enabling it to produce clear pictures of the planet's surface at night. But it doesn't work through cloud coverage. The apparatus that houses the light looks just like it and is called the candle. So, I think the Waxster knows of this which is why he says, "The clouds always dim the candles," knowing he wouldn't be tracked at night or day through the cloud coverage, and by saying, "The clouds always dim the candles," he's either laughing at us or taunting us, or both," she said.

"Thank you, Hilary, you're great, I mean really great, you just gave me an idea to check on. If you ever need anything, you make sure to give me a call; thank you." I said.

"Will do— definitely will do," she said, looking at me over her shoulder as she walked away. I looked at her ass, her face. She saw me looking at her ass, smiled, and put a more pronounced sway in her hips as she walked away. As I started tapping away at the keyboard, trying to bring ideas to fruition, I was thinking of Hilary Eubanks. She wasn't as pretty as Katherine Moore, but she was definitely plowable. Katherine was in Kansas. I might let her ride shotgun before I left.

* * * * * * * * *

I was at my terminal for three hours, tired and bleary-eyed, before I hit pay dirt. I noticed it on my screen several times before realizing its significance. It was a plane. It only appeared three times through breaks in the cloudy cover. Each time it appeared it was in the vicinity of the staging area of one of the victims. I replayed the footage on each of the planes, and it turned out to be the same one. I took the call sign. It was a twin-engine turboprop D.C 10; I closed out that screen, used my security clearance code, and accessed the F.A.A.'s database, and went to work and found what I was looking for.

The plane was registered to a Romanian business named GlobeTech, owned by Radovan Kevorkian. Further digging revealed that Globetech sold from metals to chemicals, plastics to paper and wax. They sold them wholesale to other companies. They had a long list of holdings here and abroad. They owned at least two funeral homes in every state. They were run by a nephew named Leslie Kevorkian. Further digging found that Leslie Kevorkian was none other than the son of Jack Kevorkian, the infamous suicide assist doctor. This put him at the top spot on my short list of candidates as the Waxster.

I didn't have evidence against Leslie Kevorkian, so I couldn't put him under surveillance. I needed something tangible to connect him to the victims. I started digging again.

****

The box opened, and immediately, the bright lights assailed her eyes. She blinked furiously, clearing her teary vision, and saw that she was strapped down in an almost upright coffin. She was in some sort of sterile room, and off to her left, she could see a big diamond-shaped open-topped cage. It was gleaming as though it had just been polished. She recognized what it was and who would use such a thing— she'd seen the news reports and followed the cases closely. The Waxster. He had her. She didn't cry or scream out; she knew that would be useless— a waste of energy. She was smart enough to know that weirdos thrived on fear. She decided she would show no fear—just the opposite— the lust for the kill.

* * * * * * * *

I finally figured out how he was picking his victims. Within the last five years, every single one of them had attended the wake of a funeral, or both, at one of the Kevorkian funeral parlors. He either saw them there or got their names from the sign-in books regularly kept and then given to the families so they could know who came to share in their grief. Now all I had to do was get some physical evidence, but with what I had now and no definite place to search, no judge would give me a search warrant, so I would do it the unconventional way; after all, I am a spook, and everyone knows a spook doesn't exist.

"Must you wear that silly mask?" asked the ballerina Judith McKenzie.

"I am Anubis," said the Waxter.

"Do you want some of this pubis, Anubis?" asked Judith.

"I am Anubis— I'm here to escort you to the underworld."

"I'd like to escort you to my underworld," said Judith giggling. The Waxster, Anubis stood stock still and a little dumbfounded, looking at Judith, thinking this one was different. "You are not afraid to cross over to the underworld?" asked Anubis strangely, tilting his head to the side.

"No, we all have to go some time. Your time is near; you too will have to cross over to the underworld, are you afraid?" said Judith.

"I am Anubis; I am all that was, all that will be— I am immortal."

"Are you afraid of me? —if not, why do you hide your true face behind that silly mask?" asked Judith.

"I am Anubis—I am fear," he replied.

"I've killed before— I know no fear, I'll kill again for you and with you— if you let me," said Judith.

"You're a ballerina—I am Anubis," he said.

"Yes, I am a ballerina— but I am a killer like you— you are afraid that I kill better than you, aren't you?" asked Judith. He looked at her. He was standing with his hands behind his back and brought them around the front. He had a syringe in his right hand. He looked at it, then her, stuffed it back in his lab coat pocket and turned and walked away.
"And take off that stupid mask when you come back and bring some food— pork chops— I'm hungry!!!" She yelled at his retreating back.

* * * * * * * * *

While the Feds and local police forces were doing their investigations, legally, we at the C.I.A. operated clandestinely to get the results desired and now was such a time. I sent a bulletin to all our field agents and offices and safe houses nearest the funeral homes belonging to Kevorkian and ordered them to surveille the premises, and as soon as darkness prevailed and whoever was working went home, the premises must be breached, and photos taken strictly on a fact-finding mission. Meanwhile, I sought to locate Leslie Kevorkian. I put an A.P.B. only to our garrisons with the express order to locate and surveille only. I then got on my computer to locate his airplane, figuring he wouldn't be far from it.

* * * * * * * * *

Judith McKenzie knew instinctively that she had bought herself some time by acting the way she did and decided to keep it up and did.
"If you let me out, I can show you several poses that you could enshrine me in," said Judith, "And didn't I tell you I wanted Pork Chops? —thanks for the franks anyway; they're making me think of yours— will you let me taste yours before I die? If so, I'm ready to die now."
"Are you really ready, Judith?" asked Anubis.
"Yes— we all have to go some time; I know this, you know this, but deny it, your time is near also," said Judith.
"I am Anubis— I am immortal— I will make you immortal for all the world to see Judith McKenzie."
"Are you going to give me your frank before I go, Anubis?" asked Judith. Judith couldn't see his facial expression behind the mask, but if she could, she would've been happy because Anubis visibly blanched, turned and walked out again.

* * * * * * * * *

Transylvania, Romania 43 Years ago:

Six-year-old Leslie Kevorkian ran as fast as his little legs would carry him, knowing he would be caught, eventually. He heard the rustle of footsteps and just as he was about to look, rough hands snatched him up roughly off his feet. He fought wildly again in vain trying to break free but couldn't do it, he was brought back to a clearing in the woods at the base of the mountains and thrown roughly to the ground in the middle by the stone altar. He looked at the circle of masked faces, waxed mask faces. Some were of dogs of different breeds, some cats, some bats, some pigs, his heart beating wildly in fear. The people of the mountains had caught him again.

"Do you choose life or death?" said the speaker with the pig mask, who led the procession and waited. Little Leslie didn't reply out of fear.

"Well," asked the speaker and when no answer came, they picked him up and stripped him, laid him on the stone altar on his stomach.

"If you choose death, you die and live in damnation forever and a day." Then the one with the bat mask came over with a riding quirt and a see-through mask of a jackal.

Then the rest of them came over and raised their quirts over their heads and little Leslie screamed: "I chose life!" The quirts lowered slowly. Two cat masks stepped forward simultaneously as the rest stepped back. Both had two candles—one small thin one appx. 5" long, and one long one appx. 12" wide. Each took a small candle and stuck it in his ear and lit it, the others standing back started chanting, "Anubis-Anubis-Anubis," The cat mask then stuck one of the big candles in his mouth and one in his ass roughly. Leslie moaned in pain. They lit the candles and then started pushing them back and forth slowly. The whole congregation took turns doing this until the small candles burnt down, then they stopped pushing the big candles in and out and sat down lotus style around the altar as Leslie lay there and drank down merlot till the big candles burnt down. Once the candles were removed Leslie was roughly sat up and bat face came over to him with the mask of the jackal. "You are Anubis— lord—keeper— escorter to the underworld. If you do not wear your mask on the trails again you will die— do you Understand Anubis."

"Yes," said little Leslie.

"Do not forget," said bat face, and he didn't.

The faint shrill call got little Leslie up and he snuck out of his house to his stash spot and retrieved his jackal mask and went to the shrine. They were all there waiting, and he had to submit unequivocally to the deviant rites of his forced congregation. Even though he'd gotten used to the abuse he was still scared of them. Leslie would always be in fear of them — women.
"You've successfully completed your rites of passage Anubis. You leave soon for the new world. Carry on our tradition or we will come for you, do you understand?" said a cat mask face. "Yes," said little Leslie. The congregation took off their masks in unison and looked at Leslie earnestly, they were all women.

* * * * * * * * *

Judith McKenzie was a smart girl. She realized immediately that the Waxster became flustered to the point of uncertainty when she spoke raunchily to him. She felt that was the reason she was still alive. So, she decided to keep it up. Maybe she could eventually talk him into releasing her or prolong her death till she could be found by police. They would be sure to be looking for her by now.

The Waxster had removed her from the coffin. She was now in the middle of the room tethered to the floor by a seven-foot-long chain that ran from a thole in the floor to her neck. The Waxster stood just out of arm's reach of her holding a syringe that was at least 7" long and looked deadly.

"How about this pose?" said Judith and then did a handstand and slowly spread her legs until they were completely separated in a perfect open pair of scissors. "Your candles would stick up perfectly from out of my pussy and ass, and my mouth and ears," she said and watched as he shifted from feet to feet, as if unsure about something. "Come over here and eat my pussy first— I want my pussy eaten before I die," she said.

"I am Anubis," he replied standing there looking at her stoically.

"Come over here and eat my pussy Anubis," she yelled at the top of her lungs. The Waxster took a step back, turned and left with haste.

* * * * * * * * *

"Preliminary reports from our penetration teams confirm that he's definitely our guy," I said, passing the file folder across the desk to director Foss.

"It's all there, in every one of the 26 funeral parlors back rooms, or basement, hair samples or a fingerprint of one of the victims was found," I said.

"It would be thrown out Willis, illegal search and seizure," said Director Foss.

"That's easy to get around, in the course of the arrest he resisted and was killed accidentally," I said.

"We need to take him alive and put him on display, alive Willis, and legally," said Director Foss.

"Yes, sir," I said and left.

After the gulf war "ended" and army surplus was sent back home I procured a hummer. I then had it hooked up. It was a real hummer, not the model sold by domestic dealers. I had it repainted all black with black tints, black alloy rims, and it bristled with antennas. I also had the engine doctored by a dragster pit crew. My hummer looked and acted just like it was supposed to be, a beast!

It was Mason and Bennett and me. We were on board a company C130 Hercules troop transport which I was flying and in the back was my hummer and we were heading for New York, where Kevorkian's plane was at, LaGuardia AirPort. While enroute I had

Bennett check on the computer bookings for burglaries and also the name and address for McCall's funeral home in the Bronx — Kevorkian's place.

"Robert White, I have a deal for you," I said. "My name is Dexter Tisdale, Homeland Security," I showed him my I.D. He looked at it nervously.
"I want a lawyer," he said.
"You do not need one for this offer I have for you," I said. He looked scared to death. "You're currently charged with burglary 3rd, you have two felony convictions for burglary—this will be your third making you a predicate offender, which will make you eligible for a life sentence. Do you want that?" I asked.
"No sir," he responded meekly.
"I wouldn't either if I was in your shoes. If you do as I ask your current case will be dropped to a misdemeanor," I said.
"What do you want me to do?" he asked.
"Break into McCall's funeral home. Trip the silent alarm, the cops will come and arrest you, this case will also be dropped to a misdemeanor, and I will make sure you get no more than 60 days county time for both issues," I said and pushed the paper with the terms of the agreement on it. "You can't beat it," I said.

"What's going on at the funeral home?" he asked.

"You'll read about it in the papers and hear about it on the news— now sign— time is of the essence," I said, and he signed. "Go and trip that alarm— be sure to be inside," I said and nodded to the officer in the room and he uncuffed him and escorted him out.

Forty-five minutes later two things happened simultaneously. The first was the silent alarm went off for McCall's funeral home, and the second was that Jacques Novak was ushered into the same interview room and cuffed to the desk.

"Mr. Novak, I am Special Agent Dexter Tisdale, Homeland Security," I said.

"I'm here legally," he said.

"Never said you weren't," I replied.

"Then what do you want— I've committed no crime," he said.

"I beg to differ, I think you're aiding and abetting in kidnapping and murder," I said.

"I don't know what you're talking about," he said.

"I think you do," I said.

"I want a lawyer," he said.

"Only the guilty say things like that Mr. Novak," I responded.

"If I'm not being charged with anything I'd like to be released immediately, I know my rights- I'll sue," he said. I leaned over and opened the bag and pulled out a dress, purse and shoes and put them on the table between the two of us.

"Looks familiar?" I said. Beads of perspiration broke out on his forehead.

"I want a lawyer," he said.

"When a suspect requests a lawyer all questioning must cease, so I will not ask you any questions, but I can still tell you something you might find interesting. These items of evidence belong to Judith McKenzie, who is from Roxbury Mass., who has been missing now for three weeks. They were found at your place of employment. Also, found at your place of employment were articles directly associated with the serial killer known as the Waxster. Personally, I do not believe you are him but if you do not help me out the D.A. is going to throw all of this on your lap. 27 counts of premeditated murder, across state lines, equals lethal injection at the federal penitentiary at Terre haute Indiana. You'll be able to see the cell that Timothy McVay was in. If they don't get you for the murders, they most certainly will get you for aiding and abetting in the kidnapping of Judith McKenzie because your house is being searched as we speak and if you don't help us out here, I'll tell the D.A. that these article of Judith's right here were found in your basement," He put his head down in his hands and after a couple of minutes said, "How can I help you?"

"Where is your boss, Leslie Kevorkian?" I asked.

* * * * * * * * *

The Jackal walked in this time with determination and Judith, even though she was scared to death, fell straight on her back and spread her legs wide with her ankles towards the ceiling and said: "I knew you'd be back to get some of this pussy, I'm going to die happy knowing I got some dick before I died," and used her fingers and spread her lips showing the hot pink opening to her insides. "Come and get it — this pussy is yours!" He stopped dead in his tracks looking down at her pussy and for the first time in a long time he broke out in a sweat of fear. As the memory of the last time, he saw such a pink vagina, staring him in the face.

Transylvania, Romania: 43 years ago:

When the congregation took off their masks showing them to be all women, little Leslie went livid with fear. Two of them snatched him up and laid him on the altar and securely tied him down roughly. Once that was done one took a heavily burning log from the fire, another stripped down and climbed up on the altar with her legs wide open right over his face. Another put her face next to his and showed him what he later learned was a scalpel and said; "It's time you became one of us." The one standing above him squatted down holding her vagina open with two fingers and that's when he saw the hot pink opening for the first time. "Whenever you see this," said the one with the scalpel, pointing it at the pussy of the girl squatting over his face "Always remember the pain and equate it with the power of the pussy." He then felt her left hand pull his dick upward and the searing pain as she sliced off his dick. He screamed out in pain with all his might, but the screams died out immediately as he fainted when the girl with the burning wood pressed it against his dick to cauterize the wound.

* * * * * * * * *

Woodlawn Cemetery is a sprawling affair. Just standing outside of it looking in gave me the creeps and I didn't like it or the feel of the night. Me, Bennett, and Mason scaled the fence and moved inwards. We took separate trails to cover more ground.

According to Jaques Novak, one of the mausoleums towards the middle held a door leading down into the ground about 100 feet down. At the bottom was a labyrinth of rooms adjoining each other, branching out in all directions. They entered the mausoleum and checked, and it was what we were looking for. We found the doorway that was cleverly concealed. A row of stacked tombstones was actually a door.

We entered with guns drawn and flashlights off and made our way down. Once in the main room we branched out to search. I came to a room that had another door that led to a fully operational galvanizer for chrome steel. The next room was a storage room full of metal slats and bars and rods. One room opened up wider than the rest and contained waxed caged statutes of animals. All kinds. The sculpting itself was mesmerizing. The man was talented, no doubt about that, but he used it the wrong way. It was a shame dementedness reigned supreme in the mind of Lesie Kevorkian, I guess like father like son. I came to a lab with all manner of machines and gadgets, looked around slowly panning my flashlight. I saw what I thought was a statute, but when I got closer, I realized it was a person, a girl. I reached down while looking at a door on the opposite side of the room feeling her wrist for a pulse. When I touched her neck, her eyes fluttered open and looked at me widely, then she jumped up amazingly quick and wrapped her arms around my neck tightly.

"Where is he and are you okay?" I said.

"He went that way," pointing towards the door. "And yes, I'm okay. Can you please get this chain off my neck and get me out of here?" she said holding on to me like she was a wrestler trying to submit me.

"Only if you let go of me," I said, and she did.

"Get dressed, how long ago did he go through the door?" I asked.

"About 20 minutes," she answered.

""Get dressed and go that way," I said pointing. "Yell out 'Mason' or 'Bennett,' they'll find you, I'm going after waxy boy," I said and went through the door.

* * * * * * * * *

Leslie was looking down at Judith playing sleep when the alarm lights flashed, he popped open his laptop and saw the three men enter the mausoleum door armed. He grabbed up what he could and took off through his secondary entrance and left, he headed straight for LaGuardia airport.

The door I went through led me to a series of other doors that led me to a tunnel that led me outside through a tombstone door. My hummer was a half block away and I raced to it and got in and jumped on the Bronx River pkwy headed to LaGuardia. The hummer was fast as hell, and I had to check my G.P.S. to see the twist and turns up ahead from the unfamiliar highway, then I radioed logistics and had them ground all flights out of LaGuardia immediately, then I radioed the state troopers and let them know I was coming through so they would not stop me.

The Humvee was flying. I pulled up the Kevorkian file on my dashboard computer and scanned it looking for vehicles and noticed he kept a twin-engine Cessna, at Kennedy Airport on Long Island. I changed my mind and headed there instead and called up logistics again and had them ground all flights out of there too.

As soon as Leslie Kevorkian was about to enter the airport parking lot, he saw the parade of bustling police activity everywhere and went right on by and made a beeline to Kennedy Airport instead—plan B.

When I got to Kennedy airport, I flashed my N.S.A. badge and entered. I drove straight to the runway and headed to the plane parking area. When I got there, I quickly located his plane, parked behind another plane, two planes down, and went and boarded his plane and waited.

Leslie Kevorkian was a happy camper. There was no police activity at all as he arrived at Kennedy Airport and he quickly and easily passed through the checkpoints, parked and walked towards his plane. When he got to about 5' from the door it opened, and the stairs folded down neatly, and a man stood just inside the door and stepped out. Leslie stood frozen in shock and didn't know what to do.

When I stepped out of the plane, I wasn't expecting to see what I saw. A woman stood before me, an elegant woman. She had long wavy jet-black hair, big soulful eyes, and lips, she had on a red silk spaghetti strap dress with matching shoes and purse and a large duffle bag, she looked like a wild gypsy woman, a rich one.

Leslie looked at the big man standing on the fold downstairs of her plane and thought he must be at the wrong plane. The man was big. He was well built and looked strong, very strong.

"Who are you?" asked Leslie very femininely. I looked at this obviously cultured lady and said to myself, "Who the fuck is this and where is Kevorkian?" I then looked intently at the face and realized this lady is related to Kevorkian, she had to be, she looks just like him.

"I think I have the wrong plane ma'am, I apologize," I said. Leslie Kevorkian said to himself, "You're at the wrong place at the right time mister, you're going to be my next victim you big handsome brute you."

"Oh, it's quite alright, it's not every day you meet the potential man of your dreams waiting for you at your plane," said Leslie with a smile. "what's your name big boy?"

"Dexter, and yours?" I said.

"Leslie," she said, "would you like to have a drink with me before I take off?" I was stunned.

"Leslie Kevorkian?" I said and as soon as the words left my mouth Leslie dropped the duffle bag and lunged at me with a syringe like a fencer. I jumped back deftly avoiding the point and threw a weak jab that clipped him in the mouth. It wasn't a strong blow because I was jumping backwards and he was lunging forward, but it had enough zeal on it to buss his lips, they became instantly cherry colored and began bleeding freely. Leslie stepped back and kept feigning back and forth trying to stab me with the syringe, but I bobbed and weaved the lunges, avoiding that point. "Put it down Leslie, don't make me hurt you," I said, and Leslie responded with more bass than lurch, "You're going to be my next victim," and lunged viciously at me. I knocked his hand to the side and caught him with a straight right that split his cheek bone like it was chopped with an ax. Blood ran down his face in a stream. He put his head down and charged forward throwing an overhand right, I quickly took a step back and pivoted to the left and caught his overhand right— right at his wrist with both my hands and pulled him towards me and came up with a knee at the same time that caught him in the forehead and dazed him completely. He flew straight back, and his wig flew off his head straight behind him and landed on the tarmac a few feet away. When he hit the ground, he landed flat on his back and hit the tarmac with a loud thud, he was out cold. I dragged him to my hummer and put him in the back and cuffed his knees to the floor, his hands cuffed behind his back, and his neck cuffed to a specially welded back bar specifically made for that purpose. I called airport security and had them secure the plane and took off for F.B.I. headquarters in D.C., in my Humvee, it was going to be a long drive.

* * * * * * * * *

When I reached D.C., it was all over the news that the latest victim of the Waxster had been found alive, and that authorities were actively seeking Leslie Kevorkian, the Waxster, who was still at large. I had on my radio listening in.

"You hear that, Leslie? they're looking for you all over and here you are spending quality time with me, how about that huh?" I asked. Leslie was in the back seat in shambles and didn't even speak, just bobbed his and weaved with the jolts and bumps of the ride like he was drunk.

"So, tell me Leslie, when did you first feel the sensation of euphoria from a candle going up your ass huh? I know you had something up your ass that burned slowly, which is why I believe you put the candles in your victims' asses. That theory also coincides with the dress you are wearing, which incidentally is very fetching. When did you get your tranny operation? You know, if you would have walked on by the plane, you'd have gotten clean away because I really thought you were a man— a sick delusional man— but a man nonetheless, but instead you try to emulate a woman. But to give credit where it's due, you spent your money well, because you damn sure look like a girl. But you're a lucky bitch. You're lucky because my boss, as well as the president, wants you alive— and that's the only reason you are alive cause I'd prefer to kill people like you. You killed 27 people in the act of living out what you thought or whatever," I said and swung a back hand without even looking and slapped the shit out of him.

Connor Rawlings was pissed. He was mad clear through. He was mad because word on the wire was that The Waxster's latest victim was found alive and well by Special Agent Dexter Tisdale of Homeland Security, a.k.a. Willis Dash, the spook. Also found were all the layouts and how he chose and secured and transported victims. But for some reason they couldn't locate Agent Dash after he took off in pursuit of the fleeing suspect and he wasn't responding to hails. Special Agent Conner Rawlings knew that the events of a young Willis Dash's life led him to be the way he was, and he couldn't hold that against him, but he believed the animosity between the two was because of the beautiful Katheryn Moore.

Connor Rawlings stood at his office window with both hands on the windowsill looking out thinking these thoughts and

thought to himself it wouldn't be bad if Willis, in the pursuit of the Waxter got himself killed when he seen a big black on black hummer— definitely army surplus— come speeding down the street and skidded violently to a stop with two D.C. metro police cars close behind, in front of the J. Edgar Hoover building. The door flew open and out jumped Willis Dash. He adroitly opened the back door, stuck his head in for a minute, and as the police cars screeched to a stop, he threw his prisoner out face first in front of the police car, it almost hit the prisoner. Connor Rawlings then watched as Willis grabbed the leg irons and dragged the prisoner toward the entrance with his face scraping along the ground. He realized with a shock that the prisoner was a woman. Her dress was blowing in the wind revealing pink panties. As he watched, the woman's face was hitting every step of the stone's stairs. Willis entered the lobby, and everyone stopped to look at him and what was going on. The security officer ran from behind the desk over to Willis who was headed towards the elevator.
"Hey, you can't do that here, stand her up," he said as Willis approached.
"I can do what I want," said Willis.
"That's brutality, we're the feds, we don't do that here," said the guard. "You're on camera."

Willis ignored him and when he got to the elevator, he stood there calmly waiting for it with his foot on the Waxster's neck, and looked down at him and said: "You hear that, Leslie? You're on camera. Your makeup is a little smeared, but I'll tell you what, the blood on your eyebrows and cheeks matches your lipstick perfectly." Willis literally threw Leslie Kevorkian through the situation room's door. He flew in— hit a desk, rolled over and hit his face on a computer screen breaking it, then fell off the desk and hit his jaw on the side of the adjoining desk breaking that with an audible pop. Connor Rawlings ran in from his adjoining office and stopped and looked at the scene like everyone else.
"Ladies and gentlemen, at this time I would like to introduce you to the Waxster." said Willis and kicked him in the stomach and stomped on his head a couple of times, "Would someone be kind enough to take him to booking? because if I have to do it, he probably won't make it alive, and yes," I said "she is a he!"

"Special Agent Connor Rawlings, I would like you to take this collar," I said as we sat down face to face in his office.

"Why? you did all the work and deserve the accolades it entails for bringing in such a wanted, ruthless deviant," he said.

"Why do you ask? For two reasons Connor, the first is simple, there is no person named Special Agent Dexter Tisdale of Homeland Security," I said.

"You could have fooled me. That I.D. you have is genuine," he said.

"You know I have access to any I.D. I want to. Plus, even though we don't get along I think you're a good person and could go far up the ladder especially with a collar like this one, and in the interests of national security, you know spooks should remain ghosts, we're more effective that way in neutralizing threats," I said.

"Thank you for the compliment, Willis, and in the interests of national security I will do it because I know that if I don't, I'll be getting a call from the president advising me to do so, what's your second reason Willis?" he asked.

"Katheryn Moore," I said. He looked at me and I could see the anger rise in his face and that's just what I wanted, and I rubbed it in his a little more. I pulled out my cell phone and hit the speed dial and put it on speaker phone.

"Hello, who's this?" said that sweet voice of hers.

"It's your fiancée," I said, and she giggled lightly. Connor Rawlings was furious.

"Funny, I don't see anything on my finger," she said.

"You will when I get there, what you got on?" I asked.

"I'm just like my ring finger, naked," she laughed.

"Be there soon, baby," I said.

I LIKE IT HERE

Katheryn Moore was on her way home and was looking forward to a nice quiet evening at home which was why she didn't notice the big black Humvee following her. When she finally decided it was following her it picked up speed and came alongside. Its windows were tinted, and she immediately felt that it was a law enforcement vehicle of some kind.

The big black Humvee picked up more speed and passed her and then turned in the lane she was in. She immediately memorized its plates and began punching the number into her dashboard computer. A couple of seconds later, her computer pinged, and she looked at the screen and the "Top Secret classified Access Denied," banner was flashing, and she said, "What the?" Then she smiled because she had a feeling, she knew exactly whose Humvee that was. Her phone, which was attached to her dashboard, chimed and she hit the speaker phone.
"Hello who's this?" she asked.
"Do you always check peoples' plates who go by you minding their own business?" asked the caller.
"Only when they follow me," she answered.
"I wasn't following you," said the caller. "

"Then what do you call it?" she asked.

"I was, and still am, on my way to see the love of my life," said the caller. As soon as she heard those words, she was absolutely certain who was in that Humvee and smiled broadly.

"You sound as though you really love her," she said.

"I do - from the very first time I laid eyes on her, and till this day, I have never loved another and doubt if I ever will," said the caller.

"Are you sure it's not puppy love?" she asked.

"I'm too big to be a puppy," said the caller.

"I could only imagine," she said.

"You don't have to imagine," said the caller.

"Why not? — You're obviously into her, whoever she is," she said.

"She is your lovely lady," said the caller.

"Funny I don't recall a man being in love with me like the way you say you are, and who are you anyway?" she asked coyly.

"If you say so," said the caller and the Humvee picked speed and pulled away and Katheryn Moore hit the gas but couldn't keep up. She recalled the number but there was no answer.

When Katheryn Moore Pulled up to her house the big Humvee was parked in her driveway. She pulled up behind it and when she did, her phone rang. She looked at the number and started smiling.

"Hello—who's this?" she asked, opening her car door and stepping out.

"The love of your life," said the caller. She walked to the door of the Humvee and looked in but couldn't see inside because of the tint and said: "That's news to me— can you be a little more specific?"

"Why sure— I'm about 6' tall, with beige fur, and weigh not even 10 pounds, and my name is Bruce, and I can't wait to lick your face," I said and lowered the window and the first thing she saw a cute little face of an Alsatian puppy I got from the company kennel.

"I Oh, he's so beautiful," she said and took him as I stepped out and she reached out and wrapped one arm around my neck while holding the puppy with the other and I reached down and held her waist and kissed her. We kissed long and gently, all the while the puppy was licking our chins. I knew there was no other woman in the world for me and I would never love another. We went inside and put Bruce out back and then made love all night long and, in the morning, when we woke up, I proposed to her, on one knee, and pulled out the ring I had made with one of the diamonds I recovered from the Russians. It was a 25-karat stone and I had it set in pink Panamanian gold. When she seen it, she started crying and said "Yes— Willis, I will marry you— there was never a doubt in my mind that I wouldn't be your wife, once you were old enough to be my husband," And we started kissing furiously and while I was kissing her I thought to myself that I was the luckiest man in the world, and if she thought the ring was something, wait till she saw the necklace and matching earrings and wrist bracelets and ankle chain I would be giving her as time went by.

She immediately started making plans for motherhood because she was 10 years older than I and wanted children now and that was fine with me because I wanted some too. She also planned on transferring to D.C. to be closer to me. She liked the D.C. area better than Kansas anyway. We spent the next month making plans and having sex. Six months later we were married, and I pulled some strings and got her after transfer pushed through, and nine months later she had our first child, a boy named Miles, and life was great.

THE TRADE

Most people think the entity known as the C.I.A. is America's specific intelligence agency, and it is, but the truth of the matter is it operates anywhere it pleases in order to protect American interests, that includes, American soil, like when I had to help take down the Waxster. But when it does operate on its home turf it uses so much finesse no one knows of its involvement except its assets who get the job done. That's why they are called spooks, no one knows they're around, and are responsible for what's going on or the closure to something that has come to a situation.

It was these thoughts that were going through my mind as I sat at an outdoor cafe sipping coffee waiting to make contact with the seller. I knew I was being watched, intently, and that my life hung in the balance, but I was secure in my belief and my capabilities.
"Excuse me kind sir, is this seat taken?" asked a balto clad woman, indicating the chair next to me. I was in Budapest, Hungry and the cafe I sat in overlooked the Danube. Immediately I knew this to be the contact but had an uneasy feeling about her because her accent was not of the north where we were.

"No, it's not, refined lady, you seem winded, would you like to rest for a while before moving on?" I said in Hungarian flawlessly.
"You are far too kind," she said and sat.

We sat and made small talk for a while and I detected the eastern bloc in her enunciation of certain words and phrases and knew she was Russian —probably rogue K.G.B. because that's the only explanation for what she was selling, otherwise she would be giving it to Mother Russia, not the highest bidder. She slid me a flash drive as she pulled out her laptop and I did the same. I booted up my laptop and waited patiently as she did the same. The only difference with mine is that I installed a scanning program as part of its boot up procedures which scans and copies any and all computers near it, and once completed it gives the all clear sign and powers boots up all the way. So, while she typed in her access codes, my computer copied them, and everything on her drives.

I inserted the flash drive she gave me and looked around vaguely, keeping an eye on her security details that thought they were unnoticed by me and mine. I looked at the schematics briefly from the flash drive and knew exactly what and where I was looking at and nodded to the woman with a smile of approval. I unhooked the flash drive, pocketed it, closed my laptop, and turned her laptop around towards me and typed, and a few minutes later, the words "Wire transfer complete," flashed back and forth on the screen.

"Nice doing business with you," she said as she closed her laptop and started to get up to leave.

"I would be interested in missile technologies also," I said.

"I'll keep that in mind," she said looking down at me.

"Please do, as you can see, I pay well," I said. She spun without a backward glance and left. I sat right where I was and watched as she filtered out and disappeared, then I too, disappeared.

****

Langley; 3 Days Later:

In the conference room was me, Director Foss and several others including Mason and Bennett. I turned on the large screen and it showed the extensive blueprints of our newest nuclear-powered submarine, "The Isis."

"As you all see, it is our newest attack submarine, The Isis, when it was at port in Seattle, Washington, two months ago. I did a little digging and found out that said subs first patrol was from that port and she's still out to sea as we speak."

"This picture here," I said and changed the view, "Was taken right at the entrance mouth to be the base. How the navy could let anyone get that close to take these pictures is beyond me unless they were taken by, and passed on, by one of us. This we must find out immediately."

"Secondly, is this," I said and hit the button and the picture changed to a split screen of England and America with red dots indicating different locations. "The red dots are locations of areas which were bombed recently, here and in the U.K. I got them off of the computer of the seller which accepted our money for the blueprints, which means they are connected. They've sent extortion notes to stop the bombing to both our presidents.

"Also, stopping the bombings should be relatively easy, as also on the drive are the location, I believe of the next intended targets," I switched the screens and other locations highlighted in yellow appeared. "I've forwarded the U.K. locations to our asset there who will forward them to M.I.6., they have to handle things on their end."

"I will be notifying the F.B.I. myself to help coordinate the capture of the person or persons responsible over here. Then I will be going overseas— me, Mason and Bennett are going to get the master mind."

* * * * * * * * *

Conner Rawlings of the F.B.I. sat in his office going over the files of the most recent bombings in Austin, Texas with misgiving. All the bombs' targets were apparently of the domestic variety and thus would be that much harder to track down. Home grown terrorists need only to access the internet to learn how to make a bomb, and it is much easier for them to access the material needed for such than a foreign nationalist on American soil. But what really worried Special Agent Connor Rawlings was the design of the bombs, they indicated a foreign hand, yet the exuberant demands were apparently domestic, in nature and intent, and that just didn't add up. Therefore, he was sure the bomber was an American who had been radicalized or maybe even a disgruntled vet who couldn't get a job and decided to kill others instead of himself. It was a shame how this country treated its veterans. They gave them a holiday, and a parade, but couldn't give them a job, a shame.

Connor Rawlings was leaning towards ex-demolitions veterans because of the satisfaction of the bombs themselves. He had his army of agents sifting through army files of demolition men who had come home within the last ten years and once a file was generated further intense scrutiny would follow. Six bombs had already been detonated in the U.S. and nine in the U.K. making this a consorted campaign against the two superpowers. Now having a general plan of action, Connor Rawlings was trying to figure out a pattern to the targets and maybe, just maybe, he could figure out the next one and catch the culprit red-handed. The public's help had been asked for and so far, none of the many tips had panned out.

Special Agent Connor Rawlings made notes and speculations and filed them all together and headed to the general conference room to discuss them and strategies, and tactics that would be used to apprehend the suspect. Joining him there would be representatives from Homeland Security, the A.T.F. and M.I.6, to discuss the situation and brainstorm. When Connor Rawlings entered the conference room his whole demeanor changed because of the one man he least expected to see, the one man who had bested him several times thus far and was apparently here to do so again. It was Willis Dash, of the C.I.A.

Willis got up as soon as Rawlings entered the conference room with his hand outstretched and said, "Good afternoon, sir, I'm Special Agent Martin Bridgewater, Alcohol Tobacco, and Firearms and Explosives, Kansas Division, glad to meet you, sir," Rawlings took his hand and shook it extra firmly wondering why the spooks continuously sought anonymity. "Good to meet you too," said Rawlings guardedly.
"When the conference is over, sir, I have some intel you might be interested in," said Willis, "The stop the bombing type of intel."
"Well step over here and let me know now what you have, Special Agent Bridgewater, this way if it is valuable, I can coordinate a plan of action, within all the agencies here, and put an end to the bombings," said Rawlings,
"Sounds good to me, here," said Willis and deftly handed Rawlings a flash drive, "You do not need to know the how's or whys because it's above your pay grade, but what you have on that drive is the locations of all the targets of the bomber or bombers. What you don't

have is which one is the next intended target, so you must surveille them all, simultaneously, with bomb squads at the ready at each site. You must not let the bomber know you're watching him or them. You must not rattle the suspect lest he turn it into a suicide mission. You must take him, or them, alive for questions. They are pawns and we need to get the king—get it?" Connor Rawlings looked hard at Willis and then nodded his head in agreement. "This will be your collar, again Rawlings, and apprehending the subject or subjects is paramount. You must not engage in a fire fight if possible, or let the subject or subjects detonate another bomb, or get away. You need to have these targets under surveillance immediately without letting on that they are being watched. Innocent lives depend on it. Me, and my people will be around if assistance is warranted."

So, having put Rawlings in a position to succeed, I took off with Mason and Bennett and headed for Seattle, Washington, to the naval base there to have a look around.

* * * * * * * * *

After clearing base security protocol, we were ushered into Rear Admiral James T.

Wellingtons office and he sat stoically and listened intently knowing he really didn't have a choice in the matter, as the Joint Chiefs of Staff had appointed us Special Investigators on the case via the president himself, who happened to be one of my biggest fans, since learning of the airplane incident, so long ago, it seemed...

With a couple of M.P.'s they gave us a walk through. Then we took a ride on a P.T. boat up and down the coast in both directions going to and fro approaching the base from different angles, all the while taking pictures with a live feed to the company on my laptop. With the help from the company computer program that would compare photographs we took with those purchased, it would determine exactly where they were taken from and even the time of day by the sunlight angle in the pictures.

The computer program did exactly what it was supposed to do, and in less than 5 minutes told me what I wanted to know. It also told me something else, that several of the photos were taken from different levels of the sea, meaning it was taken from a small boat, or so I thought. Then I looked around and saw that a buoy was at the exact distance and angle of the bobbing sea level photos. I instructed the captain to go by it again at top speed approximately 50 yards away from it and snapped some pictures of it. As we headed back to the base, I examined the photos carefully. I then enlarged it and zoomed in and saw what looked like a thin black pencil with a piece of wire at the end. Immediately requested the techs at the company to have a look at it and maybe identify it and sure enough I hit pay dirt. Our tech's had identified it as a wireless live feed camera— Russian made— and could trace its transmissions vector to an almost 5-yard certainty. I gave them the green light to do so and appraised Admiral Wellington of the situation, then Director Foss, and asked for permission to proceed and neutralize the threat as soon as the location was pinpointed. I was given the green light.

* * * * * * * *

Meanwhile the bombing campaign continued, both overseas and here. Two went off in London and one in Las Vegas. All three were indicated on the intel I gave Rawlings via the information I had stolen from the computer of the seller. I wondered idly how long it would take Rawlings to apprehend someone because if he started taking too long, I would have to intercede and I was quite sure he would not like my modus operandi. I turned my attention back to the problem I now faced. The wireless transmission was traced to an area 5 miles from the base in a semi upscale neighborhood, houses stood on both sides of a beautifully tree lined street, and I had the company there in full clandestine force taking pictures of everyone and reviewed all the information the computers pictures could dig up on all the occupants to find out exactly who's receiving the transmissions.

After two weeks of relentless digging, one house started to call me. It was the house of a Microsoft executive, Christine Manus, it got my attention because of her son Terrance. Apparently, he was mad at the world because he never knew his father, who coincidentally, was an M.P. at the Naval Base... and claimed Terrance wasn't his son... Currently, Christine Manus was distraught because she couldn't locate her son who had left home over a year ago. He was a computer science Major, Programmer and M.I.T. graduate- he wouldn't return her calls. When I checked his phone logs through the company, I saw that while he didn't make many calls his phone was in the vicinity of every bombing thus far. At this point he became my prime person of interest.

I had our tech guys jam all the phone services for all the houses except for the Manus house to see if the live feed was still flowing through, and it was, so he was our guy, his house our target. Christine Manus was immediately placed under surveillance and was at work, so I decided to make entry to her house and have a look around. Entering was easy and I made my way around and could not find any computer equipment except for a laptop that when I checked it wasn't receiving any live feed, so I continued because it had to be here somewhere. He probably had some type of call forwarder— it was the only answer— it had to be. I just had to find it, and I did.

It was in the attic. I removed the ceiling panels and instead of installation between the rafters, he had lengthwise computer screens and modems and call forwarder, so he could access the information off the drives from elsewhere without ever coming near the place, that might be the reason behind the apparent parent child conflict, it might be a ruse, with the mother fully involved. I called and got a bunch of flash drives and copied everything and even got the sim card number of the phone he used to access the computer. Now all we had to do was catch the bastard.

From the information garnered from Terrance Manus' computer, we learned that he had not only took the photos by placing a live feed camera on the buoy but had also hacked the computers at the naval station and got the blueprints for the sub, without being detected, and forwarded them to someone else here in the states, who sent them across seas for sale. I wondered who that person was and if I could figure a way out to catch them too.

So, Terrance Manus was a traitor, and our bomber, and had to be caught in the act, with a bomb or something warranting a search of his mother's house where the computers would be found and the whole thing can be unraveled from there. I forwarded a description of young Terrance Manus the traitor who was only 22 to Connor Rawlings and told him to make sure to keep it off the news wire. I took it upon myself to try and track him by the sim card with which he accessed his computers, which was only a matter of time before he did that.

****

Terrance Manus thought his disguise this time was his best yet and vowed to use variations of this kind from now on. He had made his third and final trip into and out of the federal building in Tulsa, Oklahoma. In each trip he bought a different section of the bomb and assembled it, he had to do it that way because it was just too heavy to carry in one shot. Now all he had to do was dial up the bomb, which was phone activated, and it was done. First, he switched on his phone to record the pandemonium that would ensue, focused it on the building then dialed the number and heard the huge explosion which followed and smiled satisfactorily as his phone recorded the blast, and the fall of one side of the building and said to himself, "Fuck you dad," and started laughing as he was biked away. He then called his contact to give a status report and forwarded the footage of the blast.

As soon as the bomb went off, we picked up the cell phone call of Terrance Manus and tracked him and the call and listened in on his entire conversation and recorded it. His phone then went dead but that was okay because we now had his contact number and began the process of finding out exactly who was on the other end of that line. We also knew exactly where he was going and made a beeline there, not to apprehend him, as yet, but to see who he was going to see. He was headed to **M.I.T.** We called ahead and had the company set up surveillance and had agents inside and out waiting for his arrival.

Massachusetts Institute of Technology is a marvelous institution committed to the higher learning of technologies, and in my opinion, was none greater in the Americas, and said so to my two trusted colleagues Mason and Bennett, as we pulled up in the main parking lot.

Our surveillance team said Terrance Manus checked in a cheap seedy motel yesterday and has been there all day and was currently having lunch with his old math teacher, Mrs. Decker. I cut my phone on to a live feed of the two in the cafeteria and watched silently for a few minutes processing what I was seeing. At first, I thought it was the lady I paid for the blueprints, so I put her face through facial recognition and got no match but when I put the two side by side, the resemblance was uncanny, but in the meantime the target was on the move...

Terrance Manus made a bee line to the New England Thruway. I needed to know where his stash house was at, I was quite sure he had several, but I didn't want him to know we were on to him, I should've never told the

F.B.I. though. I instructed the surveillance team to stay a mile behind and use the drone to always keep him in sight.

Terrance Manus was elated when Mrs. Decker gave him his next target, elated and anxious, and as he drove toward it, he wondered at the logistics of getting the explosives in the building, but he would figure it out a way. Mrs. Decker believed in him, loved him. He knew this because she was his first true love and always will be. He still remembered the first time he saw his sexy new math teacher and the way she looked at him — the way she walked, the way she talked, he was captivated beyond reason, and was an easy mark to turn for Mrs. Decker, who was a Bolshevik revolutionist looking to turn gullible young Americans into unwitting spies for her personal revenge against America and England. Mrs. Decker, a.k.a. "The Purple Lotus," was a brilliant radical operative with a selfish cause; her own. She was poisonous to the touch, just as the flower known as the purple lotus was, which she was named after.

Now she was out to prove a point— that she was smarter than anyone in the business- it wasn't about the money, she knew the Americans wouldn't pay, it was about the game of chaos and mayhem, it turned her on, and so did young Terrance, he was so gullible and fun, and a toy of revenge. He hated his father, little did he know that she hated him too, in fact that was why she chose Terrance in the first place, to get him back. For he had unwittingly broken her heart when he left her and married Terrance's mother — the bitch!

As far as she was concerned the purple lotus' bombing campaign was just warming up and she was getting ready to step it up another notch, the coup-de-grace would be the disgrace of young Terrance's father when it was found out that his son was the bomber and that he was stealing state secrets from the military with his father knowing not wanting to turn him in. She had it all planned out— the only issue now is maintaining Terrance's focus, he was more than willing but now he wanted to have children and that wasn't feasible, she already had her beloved daughter, Svetlana, who was becoming more and more preoccupied with money and sex, and could be the downfall of their entire network and operation.

* * * * * * * * *

Since no match could be found for Mrs. Ivanka Decker, I decided to have a closer look at her situation. First, I forwarded her picture to Interpol to see if they could dig anything up and, in the meantime, I went to her listed residence to have a look around. After looking around I found the same computer set up in the attic of her house that was in the Manus house. I quickly accessed her drives and realized that Mrs. Decker was Terrance's handler, quickly proceeded to copy her files and got everything that was pertinent to her involvement in the bombings and sat down in her living room and waited for her to come home.

* * * * * * * * *

Terrance Manus circled 26 Federal Plaza three times before heading out. He headed to Jersey, Newark, to be exact, and went into an apartment on James St. where he stood for the next two weeks waiting for a phone call that would never come. That call was from Mrs. Decker.

* * * * * * * * *

I sat with my legs crossed on Ivanka Decker's coffee table, in her living room, waiting for her to come in. In my lap was my laptop which had everything from Interpol on Ivanka Decker, a.k.a. Irena Karkanova, a.k.a. the purple lotus. A very interesting character she was I thought, she'd been wanted for several political murders and sought for questioning in several bombings in Europe, Spain and France, and had been believed dead as she had disappeared 22 years ago, and here she was.

Apparently, she had made her way to America, married a businessman, Frank Decker, and got a job teaching math at M.I.T. Her husband had been deceased now for 7 years from a car accident, but more than likely had been killed by her for whatever reason she deemed appropriate. I heard her car enter her driveway and shortly after her keys opened her locks and she walked in. She was an attractive woman and looked capable but only a fool would not see the cunningness in her eyes, the way they appraised me and hooded over in apparent womanly fear of a total stranger in her house. I knew instinctively that once she got near enough to me, she'd try to kill me.
"I have money and jewelry, take what you want, please don't hurt me," she said, acting very meek and scared.
"I didn't come here to hurt you," said in flawless Russian, removing my legs from the coffee table and putting the laptop to the side.

"Who are you, and what do you want?" she said as she stood motionlessly, just looking at me, no doubt, calculating a plan of action.

"My name is Demtri Sergov, K.B.G. I need some information," I said.

"I do not understand why the K.G.B. would want information from me, I am just a math teacher," she said in English and moved further into the room.

"A brilliant math teacher and a beautiful purple flower," I said, and she changed tact.

"What is it you want?" she asked suspiciously.

"Who inside the military is supplying you with information— we need access to him or her," I said.

"I do not know what you are talking about," she said sincerely.

"Irena Karkanova, the K.G.B. has known you were here since you arrived and we've said nothing to the Americans, we don't care, you're their problem now. We have operatives here too, we know you are the mastermind behind the bombings, we don't care, in fact, we applaud you for your cunning and I sit here today to tell you to please continue and would ask only that you chose better targets and help us get information from your military source, that source is very good. We would pay well and not interfere in your bombing campaign in a show of good faith, will you help us?" I asked.

"I do not know what you are talking about," she replied and started to step slowly forward.

"Would you prefer we ask your daughter?" I said and as soon as I did, she dropped her purse and lunged forward flicking her wrist and as she did so flinging a three-inch piece of sharpened steel. She was amazingly agile and stunningly quick. In her right hand she had another of the three-inch blades. The one she flung took me flush in the vest and it saved my life, because I had no doubt that its tip would be laced with the poisonous oil of the purple lotus, her name's sake, and so was the one which she thrust straight for my face in her right hand. She wanted to just nick me, and I would be done in a matter of minutes. I deflected her thrust sideways by knocking it with my left hand and threw a straight right at the same time. She ducked under it and threw a left hook to my balls; I turned my right thigh inwards and took the blow there and grabbed the blade hand with both of my hand and pulled her bodily towards me and momentarily released my right hand, threw an elbow that caught her in the nose as she was coming in from my pull. I heard and felt the cartilage in her nose break with the force of the blow and saw her eyes glaze over immediately after hitting her with the elbow. I brought my elbow straight down on her outstretched arm and broke it at the elbow. She dropped the blade and grabbed my shirt collar with her left hand and pulled straight back and at the same time swept her left leg forward connecting with both of mine and with the pulling of my collar, I went down. She was a wild cat, this one. With one arm broken badly, she landed on top of me, and I hit my head on the side of the couch arm. While I wasn't really hurt, I was dazed, and she then kneed me in the balls. I saw stars! She tried to shimmy off me and get to the blade, but I grabbed her by the neck with both hands and began to squeeze. She used her good arm and tried to pry my hands loose, but it wasn't working. I told her to stop, or I could kill her. She wouldn't stop but then had no choice in the matter as her face started turning blue from the lack of oxygen deprivation at which point, I loosened my grip slightly because I didn't want her dead. We maintained this stalemate position until my balls stopped hurting and I rolled over on top of her and knocked her ass out with a straight right to the chin, then I tied her and gagged her.

I made plans. At 2 in the morning the company showed up with 2 huge semis and packed and moved all her belongings quietly and efficiently to a safe house outside of Virginia. We were very careful transporting her because I knew she had that purple lotus oil on her purple nails. We taped her fingers apart and put mittens over her hands and took her to Langley for debriefing. She was blind folded the whole time and had no idea where she was or who I really was, and I took the lead in the debriefing, still maintaining the guise of the Russian.

"I am truly sorry it had to be like this, Irena, and there is still time for you to help yourself, the motherland and your daughter," I said and yanked the blind fold off her face roughly. She squinted violently and proceeded to curse me out in Russian better than any sailor could, her voice sounded very nasal because of the broken nose.

"Who are you?" she finally asked.

"I already told you," I said. I am—" she cut me off.

"You are not Demtri Sergov— I know Demetri well; you are an imposter," she said.

"If you do not tell me what I want to know I will do 3 things: first, I will torture you till you talk, and you will talk, then will I turn you over to the Americans, then have your daughter Svetlana detained— indefinitely— you know what the state prison camps are like— do you want her to go through that?" I asked.

"You will never get your hands on her, imposter!" she yelled and tried to spit on me. I weaved the spittle and slapped the shit out of her. Her head snapped back with the blow. I then dragged her over to the set up and proceeded to water board her. She was game though, I'll give her that, she hung out for half hour before finally agreeing to talk, told me everything I needed to know and once I verified what she said she'd be going to Guantanamo Bay.

****

Terrance Manus was worried. Ivanka was not answering her phone and that could only mean one of two things. Either she had been captured or she was dead, and he didn't like the idea of either. He loved her with all his heart— she was the reason he was who he was, she had made him. First, he would proceed as if she was captured, he would go below ground and then make inquiries as to her status. If she'd been captured the possibilities of her talking were low but could not be ruled out so he would stay away from home and he would go to his other stash house. He waited till two in the morning to make his move. He went to the roof and crawled along it to the lip of it and peeped up and around with night vision goggles. Everything seemed normal yet he was on edge — he was nervous. He decided to trust his instincts, he went to the very end of the roofs and went down the fire escape into a backyard then into an ally, crawled like a snake until he came to the street, and continued in the street alongside parked cars until he came to a driveway, which he went down, came alongside a house where his stashed motorcycle stood under a canopy. It was a K.Z. 1000. He undid the tarp, got on, started it up and tore ass out of there.

At different positions the surveillance team saw the motorcycle speeding away but had no idea it was their target, escaping until the next day when they were given the green light to take him, and found the house empty, that he was gone. The surveillance team had slipped up- not an uncommon occurrence, but what would young Terrance Manus do now? I thought to myself. He couldn't contact his handler, so I had the computer drives check for connecting vectors to locate his position. Getting him was a priority but getting the mole at the naval base was even more significant. But the powers that be didn't want him apprehended, they wanted the mole dead, and that told me he knew more about something else someone in a high place didn't want anyone to find out, which might happen if he landed in custody, which is why they wanted him dead.

So, an asset was dispatched to take him out. Director Foss wasn't happy about his authority being usurped and wanted to know why they wanted him dead, he wanted to know what he knew it might be useful for future reference, and ordered me to kidnap the mole, and extract the information from him before he was killed and then kill him and make it look like suicide.

Captain William Smith was shocked at the news he had just received from Senator McElroy - the purple lotus was in custody at Guantanamo Bay and was talking. They would be coming for him; he knew he must not himself be caught or taken alive. So, he packed up hastily and left the base without looking back. He went to his stash house, destroyed all computer drives, got the papers he needed and caught a ferry to Catalina Island and from there to a series of other changeovers and three weeks later ended up in Bangkok Thailand.

William Smith was rich over here in Bangkok I thought as I looked at the fist full of baht's that looked like monopoly money in my hand. His face had been pinged by facial recognition software out of Burma as he apparently crossed over to here, Thailand, a week ago.

I had to find him first before Jack Moffitt did, Jack Moffitt a.k.a. "The Wasp." The Wasp was an asset I had never met because he was stationed in Asia, as an asset, to be awakened when needed, like now. I had to be doubly careful to spot him first. It took me two weeks to get a bead on a new rich American who fit Smiths' description and went to have a look, as usual I had Mason and Bennett watching my six.

William Smith entered his seedy hotel and went straight to the bar on the first floor and got him a scotch on the rocks and downed it in one gulp, took the stairs to his room and entered and fell straight on the bed out cold. I slipped out from behind his bathroom door and immediately felt a draft from the living room terrace and knew that someone else was here as the terrace was closed when I entered, and Smith didn't open it, he went straight to bed. I crept quietly along to the bedroom and peered in at smiths' inert body on the bed and stepped in and as soon as I did, I was kicked viciously from behind right in between the shoulder blades. The blow propelled me forward straight into the wall hard. I spun around and weaved a straight right that was headed for my jaw and charged forward and grabbed dude's shoulders- he immediately fell straight back and put his foot in my stomach at the same time and flipped me head over heels and I landed flat on my back hard!

I rolled over and started to getup but dude beat me to it and threw a kick to my face, I turned my face sideways and grabbed his incoming foot at the same time pushed it straight up as I was getting up and swept him off his back foot and he landed on his shoulder blades a couple of feet in front of me and did a front flip and was up on both feet and lunged at me and had a wicked looking double edged blade about 4" long coming at me chest! I pivoted like a boxer to my left and pushed the knife aside to my right with my left hand and threw a straight right with all my might, dude ducked under it and went by me as my momentum carried me by him and as it did I got a good look at his eyes and he ran up out of the bedroom and out the terrace he came in, with me trying to keep up, but he was too fast, so I let him go and called Mason and Bennett and had them try to cut him off and went to see about Smith.

The reason Smith fell out the way he did was because he had apparently by paralyzed by the asset. On his neck was a huge red spot where he'd been shot with a drug. He was wide awake but suffering from temporary paralysis from the neck down. "Mr. Smith, I am here to help you, as you can see," I said.
"Who are you?" he asked very scarily.
"Salvation, but only if you want to be saved," I responded.
"You didn't answer my question," he said.
"And I'm not going to, but you will answer mine if you want to live," I said.
"I'm dead if I talk anyhow" he said.
"That is untrue as I have already said my actions show I can and will protect you, but only if you want salvation- now do you want it? Time is of the essence, my orders are simple, if you answer my questions, you live and will be protected, if you don't, I just leave, and you'll be dead by the end of the week," I said.
"What do you want to know?" he asked, clearly rattled and scared.
"Tell me who and how you sent the information too!" I said and he did.
"Okay, good, I believe you. Take this pill and it will reverse your paralysis in 10 to 20 minutes and we can get you out of here on your own two feet as opposed to carrying you out which would be very risky cause my

hands would be filled with you and unable to protect you," I said and stuffed it in his mouth and he swallowed it and about 2 minutes later he started convulsing and foaming from the mouth, then was dead from cyanide poisoning.

Mason and Bennett were unable to cut off the would- be assassin. But that was okay because I now knew what they were attempting to cover up with the death of Smith and his suicide would have the powers that be thinking they were safe. But they weren't. I would deal with them once I wrapped up Terrance and his handlers. From Bangkok I went to meet Svetlana, the blueprint seller, who was leery of the meet, but I assured her I had something to trade that she would be interested in.

"Well, Mr. Rokmonavic, what exactly do you think I'd be willing to trade and why?" Said Svetlana without preamble as she sat down.

"You be interested to trade me the location of the boy Terrance Manus," I said looking her dead in the eyes and she looked back without blinking and I continued: "because if you do, I'll give you the location of the 'purple lotus.'"

"I know of no Terrance Manus or 'purple lotus' as you say" she said and started to get up and leave and I said, "look" and handed her my cell phone. She took it and looked at the screen and visibly blanched, then looked back at me.

"Where in a tough business Svetlana, it can get nasty and will get nasty for the person in that picture who you know as Irena Karkanova a.k.a. "The Purple Lotus," your mother. The people who have her obviously know of you, which is why they sent me, and I am here to tell you that they do not want you, nor are they the least bit interested in you, but your mother's a different story. But, Svetlana, as bad as they want your mother, they want the boy even more and would be willing to trade your mother for him, the thing is, do you want your mom?" I asked. "Yes, but I do not know where the boy is- would 10 million in cash be enough to secure her release?" She asked. "No. The boy is somewhere in your neck of the woods. You have 2 weeks to locate the boy or else "The Purple Lotus," becomes the property of the American Security apparatus known as the F.B.I. "good day," I said and got up and walked away in the other direction and could feel her stare burning my back between my shoulder blades.

As she walked away, she pulled out her cell phone and our computer phone surveillance program got her entire phone log and traced her call and that was the entire purpose of this meeting, because there was no way we would be trading the Purple Lotus for anything in this world.

Jack Moffitt, a.k.a. "The Wasp" watched through a sniper scope from about 1500 yards off at the man who fought for Smith in Bangkok and wanted to kill him, but the mission was not the man but the woman, the daughter of the "Purple Lotus," Svetlana Karkanova. She was just as responsible for the bombings as her mother- she was believed to be the one who not only smuggled in the explosives but also taught Manus how to assemble the bombs, so she was on the C.I.A. kill list too, and was the primary target here. The wasp locked onto Svetlanas' cell phone and tracked her to where she was currently staying and set up surveillance. As soon as opportunity presented itself Svetlana would be killed.

Terrance Manus was angry, angry as hell. Svetlana had told him her mother was being held by some rogue K.G.B. agents who wanted to trade her for him- he couldn't believe she actually asked him to turn himself in for her mother- what, was she crazy? He was in Miami, in Opalaca, and decided to hit the Fed building in downtown Miami. He loaded up his car from inside the garage, strapped on his suicide vest and got in his car, the garage door slid open smoothly and he was on his way. As soon as Terrance was out of sight of the house, the Feds executed a no-knock search warrant and was in there.

Terrance Manus pulled up next to a big black Humvee on 135th and 22 avenues admiring its lines when its tinted window slid down and Terrance seen the barrel of a gun pointed at him, he hit the gas at the same time he felt the sting on his neck-he shot shot through the intersection and crashed into a row of parked cars unconscious. The Humvee followed and stopped right next to the crashed vehicle and Mason and Bennett jumped out and yanked Terrance out, cuffed him and took his cell phone and cut off his vest and threw it back in his car and then threw him in the back of the Humvee with Bennett as the rest of the Feds arrived and secured the seen. Terrance sat cuffed in the back seat, dazed, and paralyzed and knew he was in real trouble when the big fella got in the back with him and looked him square in his eyes.
"Well, well, well, Terrance," I said and slapped his head sideways, clearing his vision for him somewhat.
"That's police brutality," he screamed.

"I'm not the police," I said and slapped him again resoundingly. When he turned his face back towards me, I said "Look" and showed him my cell phone. "It's your girl and she's all tied up at the moment," On the phone screen stood a picture of the Purple Lotus.
"Never seen her before," he said.
"Really? For some reason I was under the impression that she was your math teacher at M.I.T." I said.
"I want a lawyer," he said.
"You're going to need one even though it won't do you a bit of good," I said and took him to the fed building and turned him over to Conner Rawlings.

* * * * * * * * *

The real Dimitri Sergov met with Svetlana Karkanova in Gorky Park on a cool, seasonable evening. They sat on a bench.
"...Find out who has her and get her back and I'll do as you wish...," said Svetlana.
"I'll look into it immediately," he said as a patron walking a poodle came walking up with a newspaper under one arm, and sat on the same bench for a few minutes, then got up and proceeded to walk on by and when they did they put their right hand in between the newspaper being held under the left arm and a low pop sound came twice as two

silenced rounds killed Svetlana and Dimitri right where they sat. Both had been shot one time right between the eyes. Jack Moffit sauntered nonchalantly away with the poodle and headed back to the safe house, later to be whisked out of the country as the K.G.B. would be pissed as hell at the loss of one of their top agents.

* * * * * * * * *

 The $5000 dollar plate dinner at the Bistro in Manhattan was packed with the elite of the intelligence community and congress as well. Connor Rawlings was having a ball basking in the glory of pats on the back because of the successful closure of the recent bombings and he had to admit to himself even though he disliked Willis, without him he would've never caught the bomber or the Waxster, and just as he was thinking that maybe Willis wasn't such a bad guy at all, he seen him enter and immediately got angry because the beautiful Katherine Moore was with him and on his arm. He also spotted director Foss and soon they approached him. He stood with a glass and the girl he was talking to was getting angry at his obvious preoccupation with the approaching trio, finally they were all together and director Foss made introductions, but even before he did Willis recognized the eyes of the girl with Rawlings. She recognized his face first because he was the first man ever to best her in the field, and they were both shocked when the realization came to them both that they both worked for the company. Rawlings was in shock at the diamonds that adorned Katherine Moore's wrist and neck, ears and especially the huge engagement ring and wedding band that matched the one Willis wore. Director Foss said: "Willis, this Jackie Moffitt - Jackie, Willis Dash," the two stood silently looking at each other as Foss continued, "Jackie, this is Katherine Dash, Willis' wife and director of Homeland Security," They exchanged pleasantries.

"So, you two are married?" asked Rawlings incredulously. Willis looked a t Rawlings astonishment and laughed inwardly and decided to rub it in, "yes, that's usually what happens when the best man wins," he said. Kate squeezed his hand gently, meaning for him to stop, Rawlings just looked on wordlessly. Jackie Moffitt A.K.A. "The Wasp" was in a quandary. She knew she was in a situation. She had carried out a failed unsanctioned hit and this man was the reason she had failed, Senator McElroy was here, she needed to find him and let him know immediately, she begged off from Rawlings saying she had to use the bathroom so she could go find him and left. Willis gave her a head start and then went after her to see if she did indeed go to the Senator who Smith had implicated in smuggling secrets for money.

"He's here," said the Wasp to Senator McElroy as she walked up, "And he's a company man."

"Who's here, Jackie, and why should we be worried?" asked the Senator.

"The man who stopped me from killing Smith in Bangkok, and you should be worried if Smith gave you up before his apparent suicide," she said. "He's company."

"Where, is he?" asked the Senator in a more concerned tone. "That's him coming over here – his name is Willis Dash," she said. At hearing the name Senator McElroy went from worried to downright scared. This guy Dash was dangerous. He knew all about Willis and was proud to have him on the team, but he didn't want him as an enemy. His latest conquest of bringing in the Purple Lotus had made him very prestigious in the eyes of the intelligence community as well as the president. All he had to do was talk and he'll be in front of the senate intelligence committee and that's a road he didn't want to traverse. He put on his game face.

"Good evening young man, I'm Senator McElroy," he said as I walked up "and you are?" he asked with his hand extended. "Unsympathetic," I said and took his hand firmly and squeezed it hard and watched his face go from firm and committed to hurting and scared.

"I'm a United States Senator," I cut him off before he could finish and said, "Go ahead, say it again a little louder this time so we can get a good size crowd to listen in on our conversation," I said. Jackie Moffit grabbed my forearm firmly and said, "not here Willis," I looked at her and said, "You're in the same boat with this dweeb and in no position to tell or ask anything," I said Harshly.

"I was acting under orders," she replied.

"Not ours," I said and let the Senato's hand go. He flexed his fingers gingerly looking at me and said, "You're a true patriot."

"Unlike you," I said.

"I'm sure I can make it up to you," he said.

"There's no making up for treason, only owning up to it, or eating some lead jolly ranchers" I said "You have two days to pick a course of action, or else, it's my way," I said then I looked at Jackie Moffitt and said "You report to me immediately upon leaving here – don't make me come looking for you," and spun on them and went and rejoined Kate and Foss and bought them up to speed when they asked me what was that all about.

* * * * * * * * *

The next day Senator McElroy was found dead, the victim of an apparent suicide. Jackie Moffit turned herself in for debriefing and was demoted for acting outside the company and a month later disappeared and went rogue. In the ensuing operation to recover the rogue asset, three agents had been killed abroad and the asset was at large still rogue.

Jackie Moffit went rogue for real. Before leaving the company, she had memorized the kill list and was terminating targets one by one and sending proof positive of the kills back to the company. The K.G.B., the G.R.U., the East German Secret Police, and the Turks were looking for the assassin responsible for the killing of their peoples, and if they ever did catch her, and torture her and find out the Americans were responsible there's no telling how the retaliation would play out. The good thing was they all thought the killer was a man. I was tasked with finding the Wasp and bringing her back in, dead or alive, preferably alive.

Jackie Moffit was an orphan raised by the state of New York. Growing up in an orphanage had toughened her up and made her a good candidate for recruitment by the Company, who routinely sought family-less people so there would be no ties to anyone if anything went wrong. It was this reason that it would be hard to find her – there was no starting point, only the last kill, and this she would be aware of. She also knew that she could not leave any pattern to the killings cause if she did, they would surely pick up on it and find her.

She lay on the beach in Aruba in a two-piece red bikini looking at the yacht anchored not far off with her next intended target on it and was thinking of Agent Dash. He was so handsome, and strong, and was also in her eyes the smartest man she had ever met and who, undoubtedly, would be looking for here, was also the only man who had ever beat her in a fight and flash of anger crossed her eyes at the thought, and just as quickly as it came it left, for she knew better than to think in anger because that led to mistakes and mistakes was something she couldn't afford right now.

She knew, sooner or later, Dash would show up and was thinking what she could do to curtail his aggression, maybe she should kidnap his wife, the Homeland Security Director, that would cause a nice uproar she thought with a smile and would generate massive intensity to find her and that was something she didn't want.

Jackie had on big aviator glasses that hid her pretty brown eyes and had her head tilted down slightly as though looking at her legs which she was lotioning up but was really looking at the yacht and seen the target panning the beach with binoculars until it stopped at her and when it did, she opened her legs wide and started lotioning up her inner thighs. Her hope was that he'd fall for the woman alone on the beach and send someone to invite her on board his yacht, where she could poison him, but it wasn't meant to be, which meant plan B.

Jean Pierre Aristead was a Frenchman to his heart when it came to women but the pickings here were small today. He had hoped to find a nice blonde American but today it was not to be, he would have another look around later but for now he had to come to terms for his latest Business deal.

Jean Pierre Aristead was an international arms dealer and noted for not having any scruples when it came to the people, he did business with. As long as they could pay the asking price, they'd get anything they wanted and that was his downfall, it was why he was on several kill lists, but he didn't care. All he cared about was the money, and because several of his customers were influential, it was widely understood that he was not to be harmed, plus his security was up to the challenge, and not once had he feared for his life, in fact he felt he was untouchable.

Jean's yacht, the Silver Ray, was packed with people and every last one of them was drunk, or high, and partying and having a good time, as the Silver Ray bobbed lightly on the calm waters off the coast of Aruba this beautiful night. It was pitch-black with the only lights coming from the Silver Ray along with pop music, as its patrons danced, and moved around the stern and upper deck gangway. Jackie Moffitt, a.k.a. "The Wasp," stood laying on her stomach on a surfboard watching the Silver Ray, through special night vision goggles, about fifty yards off her stern. She had been there for the last two hours waiting for an opportunity to present itself and finally it did. Aristead came on the stern deck with several men looking out into the night talking. The Wasp quickly unlimbered her specially made dart rifle and took aim, all the while hoping no shark decided to take a bite out of her as she floated along.

The thing she liked most about her dart rifle was it would not release a spark when firing so no one would know what direction the shot came from, nor did it go off with a bang, just a woosh, which she was sure no one would her because of the distance she was at from the yacht, and the music being played. She also liked the projectile it fired because its point was so short that once it hit the target it wouldn't stay stuck on it, and would fall to the ground immediately, and would be hard to find unless one knew exactly what they were looking for.

She timed her shot with the swell and fired. Aristead had his back towards her leaning on the rail and shifted slightly and the projectile went right by him and hit the man in front of him in the left thigh. Jackie watched as he slapped his thigh drunkenly at the slight prick he felt, and cursing herself Jackie quickly reloaded, took aim, and fired. This time the shot went true. She seen Aristead quickly slap at his butt cheeks at the slight prick of the projectile and turned around and look behind him in her general direction, and as he did so, the first man who had been shot fell forward into Aristead, and the Wasp, as quietly as she could, paddled away.

* * * * * * * * *

"What've we got?" I asked as I entered the situation room. "The businessman Jean Pierre Aristead, number 8 on our kill list, and the Venezuelan Minister of Defense, both died of a heart attack last night on board said businessman's yacht, while partying. Our contact over there says the Venezuelans don't believe in a such a coincidence, as those two men of prominence succumbing to a cardiac event at the same time and, had dual autopsies done immediately, suspecting a drug overdose of some kind and found minute traces of cermolyperdoxim in both men's systems. Said drug is a poison which induces cardiac arrest within two minutes of ingestion, also found were areas on both men's bodies there appears to be tiny puncture wounds where said drugs were introduced into her system, they were assassinated." Said director Foss and dropped the dossier he's been reading on the table and then picked up a manilla envelope and I knew exactly who it was from before he pulled out its content. It was from the Wasp. He pulled out several photographs-8x11's and handed them around. They showed the

Silver Ray and its occupants at various angles, and the last two showed as the Minister of Defense was crumpling up going down, and the other, Aristead, in the same formation.

Everyone looked at the pictures silently for a few minutes then Mason said: "Why take out the defense minister?"
"Because he was making a purchase?" answered Bennett questioningly and everyone looked at me and I said, "Quite possibly, but I don't think so because she would know the political ramifications for such a deed, for one, and two, he wasn't on our lists, and that's all she's been gunning for, I think it was collateral damage. Shooting a dart gun from a boat or floating in water is no mean feat, with the bobbing of the swell by both boats and water. Knowing this she probably shot the defense minister by accident, then went after Aristead. In fact, one photo of when the targets went down his a small "A" in the left-hand corner of the ministers' photo, and a "B" in Aristeads photo meaning, I think, that was the order they were shot. Check eyewitness accounts and we'll probably find they say the minister went down first then Aristead." Foss tossed the folder over to Bennett who read for a few minutes then looked up and said, "Your right."

"The Venezuelans are screaming bloody hell," said Foss. "They shouldn't be trying to buy black-market weaponry," said Mason. "If they weren't this would never have happened."
"We have to find her gentlemen," said Foss.
"All things considered, she's doing pretty well for herself, and she's doing a good job,
clearing up that list for us, so why not let her continue the good work and then get her?" said agent Daniels smiling.
"Because, if she gets caught, and it falls in our lap, heads are going to roll," said Foss "Find her gentlemen, and fast, we must bring her in," and with that the meeting was over.

* * * * * * * *

Even enough it was a clear violation of company policy; I had my beautiful and extra smart wife Kate helping me locate the Wasp or her next target. Kate sat in front of my laptop banging away at the keyboard and I hoped she had better luck than I, and she did. She believed she had narrowed down the next possible two targets based on plain old fashion woman intuition and while I found it hard to believe I had no choice but to give it a shot because I was drawing blanks with my own conclusions.

"So, based on the money involved and the location I'd say that her next target is either the Swiss banker Martin Swenson, or the German drug czar Kurt Himmelstuz...," said Kate.

"So, you think we should focus on these two based on women's intuition, basically?" I replied skeptically.

"Yes, I'm a woman, remember? It's what I would do if I was her," she replied.

"Okay, love, I'll focus on the two and hope you're right," I said.

* * * * * * * * *

Martin Swenson was ecstatic. All his plans had borne the fruits of his efforts, and he was now richer than ever. Money laundering and corporate espionage was the way to go as far as he was concerned but alas, retirement was the order of the day because all money was no longer an issue, now it was time to lie in the lap of luxury and enjoy it.

He was sitting in front of his fireplace swirling his cognac thinking of the house he had just bought in the Virgin Islands and decided to sell everything and retire to the Caribbean when the new maid entered. She was a nice-looking brunette who appeared to be all business and for some reason her seemingly ignorance towards him was alluring. He liked confident women like this one, he decided that he wanted her. "What's your name?" he asked as she brought over a tray with snacks and sat them down in front of him, "Jacquelyn," she said in a slurry French accent and turned to leave when he grabbed her hand gently and said, "Why don't you stay and talk with me?"

"I do not want to get fired- your wife," he cut her off before she could finish. "Do not worry about her, sit, let's talk," he said persuasively.

"Okay" she said and sat and reached over to the tray of food she had brought in and said, "You should try this salad, I made it myself, I think it's really good," and passed it to him and he took it smiling and she smiled back as he took it and ate some and said "Yes, it tastes very good."

"I cook a lot at home, I especially like cooking poisonous mushrooms like the ones you're eating now, Martin," she said. He stopped in mid chew and looked at her hard and started feeling the paralysis setting in. He felt nausea and vertigo and fell face first into the coffee table breaking its delicate glass top and spilling everything all over the place. Jackie leaned over him and looked in his eyes said, "This is what happens to people who steal company secrets for profit Martin, they pay for it in the end - just when they think it's safe to buy a house in the Caribbean and retire, they pay for it." and watched as his body started convulsing and foaming at the mouth then died.

To disguise the motive for the murder the Wasp deftly opened the safe and pillaged it making it look like a robbery/burglary. It was a nice haul too, she got 5.7 million in cash that was already in a duffle bag and a bunch of jewelry and left.

I sat in our surveillance van watching the premises of Martin Swenson from 2 blocks away. The van was a control center for a drone, which I had flying illegally in Swedish airspace, in circles around his property. From where the van sat, I could see the front clearly through telescopic vision goggles as though I was right in front of the place. Mason and Bennett and the others were placed strategically around. As I watched I saw a man emerge from the side entrance with a duffle bag and go over to a car in the driveway, throw the duffle in the trunk, get in the car, and pull away from the house. I swung the drone around and followed the man from almost a mile behind and two miles up and recorded his route at the same time.

For the next 15 minutes I watched the house and kept an eye on the man in the cars progress, when suddenly the front door of the house flew open and men came running out armed looking around in every direction and as they did this for a few minutes I heard the chatter on the local police band to a call at the house with a fatality and to send an ambulance, I knew exactly what happened. I got on our mike and ordered everyone "Black Out," which meant clear out immediately and they did. I looked at the drone screen, at the car, and gave my driver directions and then got on the mike and gave directions and we were off in pursuit of the Wasp or a freelancer. In any event, I'd be paying them a visit very shortly. We followed the car to a small cottage about two hours' drive into the countryside and stopped about 100 yards from it. We had the entire area under surveillance with the drone and then surrounded the cottage as best we could and then I made my way on foot by myself towards the cottage for a look at the setup.

For some reason the cottage had me feeling apprehensive. Always trusting my instincts, I looked at the approaches to the cottage warily. I pulled out my cell phone and looked at the drone footage of when the man came and took the same route up to the side door as him and as I was doing so, I saw trip wires at several points off in both directions. I looked at the locks on the door and then it buzzed, startling me for a second and then I smiled knowing it was the Wasp - a freelancer would have attempted to kill me already if he knew I was on his side door. I pushed the door open slowly and peered inside warily and entered slowly into a living room, a very spacious one, and at the end, at the point where it connected to the kitchen sat Jackie Moffitt, looking at me intently. She had on a red bra and panties with fishnet stockings, her hair was long and dark brown and combed out beautifully and cascaded down and around her neck and shoulders. She was beautiful and that made her even more dangerous. She had a drink in her hand.

"So, the gig is up, heh?" she said sadly.

"I personally wish it wasn't," I said.

"If you did, you wouldn't be here," she said.

"I'm only here because you were spotted," I said.

"If you don't want the gig to be up, call in a mistaken identity, pull the surrounding troops away and let me go," she said as I came further into the room and sat across from her. She opened her legs wide and lifted her left leg up and brought it behind her ear.

"You're the only man the ever bested me and I promised myself that only such a man could get this, and the end result is I've not been fucked in twelve years," she said.

"No wonder you fight so violently, you need to get laid," I said. She giggled softly and said, "I'll go in peacefully under one condition," she said.

"You're in no position to consider conditions," I said.

"You're right, I'm in a position to get fucked and that's the condition, that I get fucked by you, if not I'll never leave this place alive, I assure you," she said and wiggled out of her panties and started playing with herself. "Hot peas and butter, come and get your supper," she said spreading her legs straight apart with ankles in the air making a perfect vee.

"How do I know you won't try to kill me?" I said, thinking to stall her because her back was against the wall, there was no getting away this time-she might snap at any moment.

"Because I don't want to kill you, nor did I want to kill the other three who initially came after me, but they were hell bent on killing me instead of bringing me in so they could pad their stats. Look," she said and showed me under her fingernail where she had a cyanide pill affixed to it. "If anyone dies here today it is me. Your orders are to bring me in preferably alive instead of dead. If you want me alive, you're going to have to fuck me first and fuck me good. I'm not going to fight you again," she said.

"I'm a married man Jackie and I love my wife dearly," I said.

"Whether you want to admit it or not your only married to your wife, you also married to the company, just like me, so you have to do what you have to do to make your marriage a happy one, so you have to make a decision on how you want to bring me in, dead or alive, the choice is yours. I will not fight you again, I know you have the place surrounded and there's no getting away this time, the only question is how I go and that's up to you, how do you want it?" she asked, fingering herself with one hand and holding the other with the pill right by her mouth.

I stood there looking at her and realized that she knew she'd be dead once in the hands of the company for killing the three agents and just wanted to get her freak off one last time and that if I did fuck her, she would kill herself anyway, so I just stood motionlessly looking on at her until she came. She rocked and shuddered with the orgasm and looked at me through lust filled eyes and stuck her finger in her mouth and ingested the pill. As I watched her go into convulsions and then pass on, I thought what a waste and called in for a cleanup crew and headed on back to the states to my beautiful wife and children and I thanked my lucky stars that I was fortunate to have such a life.

In this life nothing is promised, so I would learn in the years to come to protect my country and family in the name of patriotism. Grave challenges will take place in the name of freedoms that the company will endure clandestinely to ensure the safety of America's children and I'll be right there on the front lines with my thoughts mentally billowing in evils direction...

THE END

PAUL AND DAWN

A SHORT LOVE STORY

I've known Dawn for a long time, I considered her my best friend, and she felt the same way about me. Currently, I am involved with a girl, Kyra, and Dawn was involved with a friend of mine, Jerry. Jerry was cool but was a homebody and didn't like to hang out and Dawn did and that was leading to her discontent with their relationship.

Dawn liked to hang out and party and when she did Jerry would go home leaving her out there alone. Oftentimes I would see Dawn at a couple of clubs around the way, high as hell, hanging out with other chicks when I pulled up. So, quite naturally, we ended up hanging out a lot, after all, we were friends. Dawn was a good girl in every respect, a pretty girl, she was no whore. Everybody that met her liked her. All the fella's tried to rap to her, all the time, but she was true to Jerry, he was lucky to have her. He was her first. The problem was that he wasn't around enough, and it was affecting their relationship.

* * * * * * * * *

I came to Emma's Place, a club around the way, late one night and was chilling when Dawn came in. She spotted me and came right over, kissed me on the cheek and sat across from me in the booth.
"What's up Paul, how are you doing?" she asked sincerely.
"Nothing much boo, how are you feeling?" I asked.
"Not so well," she responded.
"What's the matter—anything I can help you with?" I asked.
"Paul, I think Jerry is cheating on me," she said earnestly.
"Why?" I asked.
"I don't know, it just doesn't feel the same as it used to," she answered.
"Maybe you should suck his dick a little harder," I said smiling.
"Paul don't talk to me like that— fuck is wrong with you!?" she said angrily.
"I was just kidding, boo, I'm sorry," I said soothingly.
"Kid with them hoes like that!" she said, still angry.
"Okay Dawn, I'm sorry, I was just trying to make light of the situation," I said. She sat there stone-faced staring at me. I got up and said, "Be right back." Left, went to the bar

and got her a drink, her favorite, Tequila, and brought it back and gave it to her.
She took a sip and looked at me thinking I don't know what.
"How are you and Kyra doing?" she finally asked.
"I'm happy, she's happy, I dropped her off a little while ago," I answered.
"Marriage in the picture?" she asked.
"I don't know, never really thought about marriage with her although I know I could do it," I said.
"Well maybe you should think about marriage," she said.
"Maybe you should too," I said.
"I am," she said.
"Good for you, Jerry's a good guy and worthy of your affection," I said.
"It's not him I'm thinking of marrying," she said with a funny look in her eyes.
"Jerry done fucked up that bad?" I asked.
"No," she said.
"Then what's the problem?" I asked.
"I think the other guy is better suited for marriage even though he doesn't realize his potential," she said.
"Marriage is a heavy step, Dawn. Do you really think that's what you need at this point in your life?" I asked.
"Every woman needs stability in her life, at all times Paul, it comes in different forms. As a

child a mother and father, as a teen a boyfriend, and good supportive girlfriends, and as an adult a husband." she answered.

"You're still young Dawn, you have plenty of time to get married and for you, unlike some women, getting a man poses no problem. You're beautiful all the way around the board, from your eyes to your personality. The moral being don't be in such a rush. Plus, you're not even sure if Jerry's cheating or not. I think something else is at play factoring in your discontent in your relationship with him, something that you're not telling me, and that's cool, you need your space, you want to work it out for yourself, I get it, you just remember this, you're my friend and I love you, I'll always be there for you know matter what, all you have to do is call me and I'll be there," I said. She blushed furiously and smiled and looked at me with a funny glint in her eyes again.

"It's not that I'm in a rush, I just don't want to let the person I have in mind get away because he doesn't know that I see him that way," she said.

"So, fuck Jerry, huh?" I asked.

"No— I just don't think he's the type to understand me and deal with me in the long term— plus like I said, I think he's cheating on me," she said.

"So, you want to be dealt with, huh?" I asked.

"I don't think I like how that sounds Paul, dealt with, it implies that I am overbearing or something," she said.

"Yes, it means that, it also means you crave more realism in the relationship. Is that the problem Dawn— he's not sexing you enough?" I said. She looked at me hard gathering her thoughts and I knew instinctively that I had hit the nail on the head and said before she could answer: "That's why you think he's cheating isn't it? He's not sexing you as much as in the beginning, so you think he's losing interest and sexing someone else." She looked at me hard again and just as she was about to answer a group of girls appeared and pulled her away to girl talk. As she was leaving, she looked at me and said, "This conversation is not over Paul."

"With women like you they never are." I responded. She laughed as they were walking off. One of the girls waved goodbye and blew me a kiss and when she did Dawn reached over to her and put her hand over her mouth and said, "Bitch don't even try it."

****

I was coming down the avenue the next day from work and as I was passing the Korean vegetable store, I saw Dawn's mother

inside and she looked out and saw me and gestured to me to come in. She really didn't have to because I would have come in and greeted her anyway because I liked her, and I knew she liked me. Dawn's mother was the splitting image of Dawn except that she was older and much thicker. Her body was fabulous. I wanted her badly! As soon as I got close enough Dawn's mother reached out and pinched my cheek fondly and said, "Hello handsome, how are you doing?"
"I'm fine, especially now that I've seen you..." I said and she smiled.
"You're so charming Paul, you should spread some of it on Dawn," she said.
"We're friends, Mrs. Griffin," I said.
"Friends make the best lovers," she responded, looking at me hard.
"Yes, I've heard that and now that you've said it, I believe it must be true for surely you wouldn't lie to me or point me in the wrong direction on such a sensitive matter," I said. She smiled beautifully at me.
"You're very well spoken and obviously my words hold a great deal of weight with you, why is that, Paul?" She asked.
"Because instinctively I know I can trust you," I said. "And besides I've been in love with you since the first time I set eyes on you, if you told me to go jump off a bridge, I'd ask you which one," I said and she laughed

lightly and moved off slowly examining vegetables as she went along, and I followed.
"Paul, if you loved me, you'd love Dawn, because we look exactly alike," she said.
"Not from the waist down you don't," I said, and she started cracking up.
"Okay Paul, you calm down now, you know better than that, you're too young for me, besides I want you for my son—in—law," she said,
"I apologize for my forwardness, and I know you'd like to see me, and your daughter hook up—you've consistently put Dawn in every conversation we've had. But Dawn likes Jerry Mrs. G— He's her first." I said, "Plus she was the one that hooked me up with Kyra—her friend."
"I'm no longer Mrs. G, it's Miss Gee from now onward, okay?" she said.
"That's the best news I've heard all year!! Now all I have to do is get rid of Kyra and we're set!" I said and she laughed sincerely.
"Paul, you're so sweet. I know Kyra and she must be about the luckiest girl in the world but too bad you're going to have to break her heart," she said,
"You're really going to get with me?" I acted stunned. She laughed even more.
"No Paul, you're going to get with my daughter," she said seriously.

"She likes Jerry miss Gee, and while I do like Dawn, a lot, I mean I really love her. I don't think it's in the cards for us we're friends," I said.
"You let me take care of her as far as Jerry is concerned, you just focus your charm on my daughter," she said with finality. The rest of the conversation was regular stuff but in the back of my mind I had the distinct impression that I was being boxed in.

* * * * * * * * *

After work the next day I was at home watching the game eating tuna melts when the phone rang. The caller I.D. told me it was Dawn. I don't know why but I was reluctant to answer it. I just looked at it like it was some kind of alien or something for a few minutes before answering it. "Hi dawn, what's going on—how are you doing?" I said speaking with more enthusiasm than I felt.
"What took you so long to pick up?" she asked demandingly.
"I was taking a leak," I said.
"Wish I was there," she said.
"Is that right?" I asked, deadpan.
"Yes, I watch you," she said.
"Voyeurism?" I asked.
"I prefer to call it marriagism," she said.

"What about Jerryism," I asked, and she started giggling.

"I told you things are not the same," she said.

"Do you have proof positive of indiscretions by him?" I asked.

"I don't need any," she responded.

"So, you're jumping ship?" I asked.

"Without a life vest," she answered.

"You'll drown or the sharks will eat you," said.

"Won't happen," she said.

"Why not?" I asked.

"Cause you're my life vest, you're going to save me and if I'm going to be eaten it won't be by no shark, it will be by you," she said laughing.

"Yes, Dawn, I would give my life for you, my friend, and I do prefer fish above all," I said continuing the banter and laughing with her.

"Yes, June is the best month," she said.

"The best month for what?" I asked.

"Don't play stupid Paul"" she said.

"I'm not playing stupid—what are you talking about Dawn? are you planning on asking for a raise at work or something, what's up?" I asked. She was silent for a moment, and I said, "Well?"

"Men are so stupid sometimes," she said.

"How can that be—we have two heads," I said.

"You only use one of them—dummy," she said, "that's why you don't know what I'm talking about."

"I don't know what you're talking about cause you're talking in riddles, and you do know why don't you?" I asked.

"Why Paul?" She asked.

"Because you have four lips," I said. She didn't laugh.

"Your nasty Paul, and why are you avoiding the subject?" she asked.

"I'm nasty? You just said if you jumped in the water sharks wouldn't eat you, that I would, and I'm the one that's nasty? you got a lot of shit with you, besides there's nothing wrong with being sexually nasty and I'm not avoiding no subject- you have yet to clarify definitively what you're talking about, you're a Riddler, a four Lipper," I said and started laughing but she didn't and I could tell she was dead serious by the tone of her voice when she said, "The subject you're avoiding is the June one, do you think it is the appropriate month?"

"Any month is appropriate if it suits your needs, but what I'd like to know Dawn is exactly what you have in mind for June that I can help you with?" I said and again she was quiet for a few minutes and once again I said, "Well?"

"They say June is the best month for marriages, Paul," she said.

"Yes, I've heard that is the case. The weather is always nice that time of year. But I do not understand why you're asking me about June, you're talking like you ain't feeling Jerry anymore and you couldn't possibly be referring to me and Kyra, because we're not that serious. Even though we've been together for almost 2 years, she's not ready for such a serious commitment, she's just not ready and I've not really given it serious thought though I know it's in my future," I said.

"If you've not thought of it seriously, how do you know it's in your future?" she asked.

"Because I want a family, Dawn, and I know I can stay put and be loyal to one because I know what it takes to do so," I answered.

"Which is?" she asked.

"Compromise," I answered.

"Please explain to me how compromise would help you stay loyal to your family—if you had one," she asked.

"Easy, Dawn, in any relationship compromise is the key factor in sustaining longevity. My grandparents were married for 50 years—till death did them part. When I was little and realized they'd been married 50 years, I was stunned and asked my grandfather how they stayed together for so long. He looked at me and said, "Compromise, son, compromise," and he wouldn't lie to me about a thing like that, and I believed him, and if he could do it, so can I," I said.

"Good answer. Paul, I have to go," she said.

"So go," I said.

"This conversation isn't over Paul," she said.

"You always say that and most conversations with you aren't, but this one is as far as I am concerned, later," and hung up before she had a chance to levy any kind of protest. She called back, I didn't answer. She texted a little while later asking; "What is a marriage ring the visual sign of?" I text her back, "Google it."

* * * * * * * * *

A couple of days later I was in the club— Emma's Place. It was about 1:30 in the morning and I was sitting in a back booth nursing a beer thinking that me and Kyra's relationship was becoming a mundane escapade, very pedestrian, all the while eyeing the girls on the dance floor when Dawn showed up. As soon as she saw me, she made a B–line straight to my booth and slid in across from me and said, "Fuck is your problem, Paul?" Dawn never curses at me.

She must be really upset with me. She had a mean little glint in her eyes too.

"What did I do now Dawn?" I asked.

"Why haven't you returned my calls, Paul?" she asked angrily.

"I've been busy, Dawn," I answered.

"Too busy for me, Paul, your friend?" She asked.

"It's not like that at all Dawn," I answered.

"Then what's it like, Paul?" she asked.

"Listen, Dawn I'm here trying to relax after a stressful couple of days at work and you're tripping over nothing and I don't think this is the appropriate time or place to have this conversation," she cut me off before I could finish and said, "Then when is Paul, because we're going to have it," looking me right in the eyes with and unblinking stare. Her arms were folded hugged close up to her breasts, and her legs were uncrossed but closed tightly. She was mad as hell at me for not answering her calls. As I sat there looking at her, I had to admit that even when mad, Dawn was one beautiful girl and I thought that maybe I should push up on her because she was obviously upset about her and Jerry's relationship and also me and Kyra's, like I said, was becoming boring, relationship wise.

I got up and slid in the booth beside her and put my arm around her shoulders and hugged her close to me and looked her in her beautiful eyes and said, "I apologize for not answering your calls Dawn, you know, and I know, and we both know that I love you dearly, always and forever." She looked up into my eyes then laid her face on my chest and said, "I love you to Paul." We stood like that, hugged up close and if anyone who didn't know us now would've seen us, they would have sworn up and down we were a couple. But I got to admit, she felt good right there in my arms, like that was where she belonged...

* * * * * * * * *

Mrs. Gee invited me over for dinner and I should have begged off, but I didn't. I should have begged off because I knew she was trying to line me up with her daughter but didn't because I liked her. I liked being around her as a person and enjoyed interacting with her immensely. She had a way of making everyone in her presence feel special and like I said earlier, her body was amazing. I could never get tired of seeing it and wondered if Dawn's would thicken out too after having a child.
"How's the food Paul?" asked Ms. Gee, as she sat down next to me. Dawn sat right across from me.

"Great, Ms. Gee, why did you think I came?" I asked, turning my head to look her in the eyes and they were twinkling marvelously. Dawn's pretty eyes were larger than usual and looked very concerned. I wondered idly at her thoughts. "Because you like being with us," answered Ms. Gee, placing emphasis on the word "us," then continued; "That you like the homey feel of the place and our presence," she said, putting a big emphasis on the word "our."

"Naw," I said smiling, "I came because I was hungry,"

"Dawn cooked," said Ms. Gee, undaunted by my denial.

"Funny I didn't see her in the kitchen," I said looking over at her.

"Well, she did, she has no problem cooking for," said Ms. Gee looking hard at me.

"Neither does the restaurant down the block," I said and dug down into the food.

"Paul, we need to talk," said Ms. Gee.

"Funny, I could have sworn you invited me over for a meal," I said.

"Seriously, Paul," she said.

"Is that right?" I responded and lifted my glass and drank some water.

"How long have you known Dawn Paul?" asked Ms. Gee, I looked at Dawn and shrugged my shoulders and Dawn answered, "We met at my eighth birthday party—twelve years ago," and looked me dead in the eyes and said, "Why are you acting like you don't know Paul?" She looked like she was about to cry, I just put my face down in that plate and started eating like a starving lion on the Serengeti.

"How old are you, Paul?" asked Ms. Gee.

"22," I said without looking up.

"I'm talking to you Paul," she said, meaning for me to look up. "And I am hearing you Ms. Gee, this chicken is delicious," I said without looking up.

"22," said Ms. Gee, "A good age to begin the foundation of your nation."

"I fail to see the relevance of that statement at this time," I said.

"The relevance being the situation between you and Dawn," said Ms. Gee.

"There is no situation between me and Dawn, we're fine," I said.

"Yes, there is a situation between us," I said to Dawn.

"Which is?" I asked.

"Me and you," she said.

"We're fine," I said.

"No, we are not, Paul," she said on the verge of tears.

"What's wrong with us? I don't know of any discrepancy in our friendship," I said emphasizing "friendship."

"Well, I do," she said.

"That's on you, as far as I am concerned, we're fine," I said.

"Paul why are you being like that?" she asked.

"Like what, Dawn? I have no idea what you two are getting at because you are obviously up to something which involves me without my consent, therefore I don't know what's going on, that's my story and I am sticking to it," I said.

"Paul, you look like a wild animal trapped in a cage right now," said Ms. Gee, laughing lightly, "You're a strikingly beautiful man."

"I feel like I'm being trapped because you two are tag teaming me for what reason I don't know," I said.

"Paul, will you please quit with the shenanigans? You're starting to make me feel like you really ain't with it and I can't bear that thought, Paul," said Dawn.

"What shenanigans Dawn? I'm dead serious, y'all are playing games and if you want to catch feelings go right ahead, it's not my fault, I don't even know what's going on," I said. I looked at Dawn and her beautiful eyes started clouding over with tears and then they started rolling down her pretty face as she looked at me miserably and I realized how much I really loved her and that she loved me back even more and that powerful feeling of love engulfed me mind, body, and soul. I got up and went around the table to her and she got up too and came into my arms and her warm body melted into mine like a sponge. She rested her face on my chest, and I said, "I'm sorry Dawn, truly I am. I don't ever want to see you or make you cry ever," She kept her face buried in my chest with her arms around my waist saying nothing.

Then she looked up at me and all I saw there in her beautiful eyes, was pure unadulterated love, and said to me "I'm not going to ask you Paul— you're supposed to ask me. I put my hand under her chin and looked into her beautiful brown eyes and said, "Dawn I've loved you from the very first time I saw you and nothing has changed except that as we grew older my love and admiration for you has grown deeper and deeper as we grew to become best friends, and as such my love, respect, and admiration grew immensely and till this day have never ever met a girl like you. I have never met a girl that I love as much as I love you. I'm sorry for not acting on it sooner and I promise you here and now that I will love you unequivocally with all my heart for you the rest of our lives, till death do us part. I promise you I'll never cheat on you or disrespect you in any way, ever. I promise you I will make you happy and keep you happy, but these promises cannot be fulfilled unless you let me fulfill them, Dawn Yvette Griffen, will you marry me?" She started jumping up and down and crying even more but this time the tears were of joy! Her eyes sparkled brilliantly with tears of joy. She took my face in both her hands and kissed me. She kissed me long, she kissed me strongly, she kissed me like no other girl ever did or ever will. She kissed me with love.

When we finally separated her mother was clapping and came around and we group hugged, and Dawn said, "Yes, Paul, of course I'll marry you, I always wanted you and always will! I promise to reciprocate your love and respect tenfold. I love you, Paul," and hugged me harder and we started kissing again as her mother stepped back and said, "Paul how's June 14th sound, it's a Saturday?"
"June 14th will be fine Ms. Gee," I said.
"Good, it's going to be great. My daughter will have a big, beautiful wedding," said Ms. Gee.
"Yes, she will," I said as we stopped kissing looking into each other's eyes.
"Yes, and I'll have those beautiful grandchildren I want," said Ms. Gee. Happily.

"Yes, y'all win," I said with a big smile on my face and was happy.
Very happy.

THE END

www.ingramcontent.com/pod-product-compliance
Lightning Source LLC
Chambersburg PA
CBHW050900160426
43194CB00011B/2223